THE
REFORMATION

Patrick Collinson

PHOENIX

A PHOENIX PAPERBACK

First published in Great Britain in 2003
by Weidenfeld & Nicolson
This paperback edition published in 2005
by Phoenix,
an imprint of Orion Books Ltd,
Orion House, 5 Upper St Martin's Lane
London WC2H 9EA

1 3 5 7 9 10 8 6 4 2

A CIP catalogue record for this book
is available from the British Library.

ISBN 0 75381 863 9

Typeset by Deltatype Ltd, Birkenhead, Merseyside
Printed and bound in Great Britain by
Clays Ltd, St Ives plc

www.orionbooks.co.uk

'Over 40 years, the history of English Protestantism has been transformed – more by Patrick Collinson . . . than by anyone else . . . This brilliant, charged little book . . . is a work of tough thinking, the late fruit of a working lifetime's reflection'

Blair Worden, *Sunday Telegraph*

'Patrick Collinson's sparkling little study . . . the first 100 pages offer a series of brilliantly compressed narrative accounts of the main strands of the Reformation – Lutheran Germany, the radical "sects", the Swiss Reformation, the British Reformations. Each is admirably done, crystal clear, pacey and with a seasoned teacher's eye for the telling anecdote or the rudest joke to ease down the diet of facts'

Eamon Duffy, *Sunday Times*

'Collinson's story is slick and amusing. The light touches he employs bring the characters to life in a way that is convincing and subtle'   John Townsend, *Catholic Herald*

'An engaging book that guides you through the happenings, interpretations and consequences of the Reformation and Counter-Reformation. Patrick Collinson has drawn together the work of generations of historians in a masterly and accessible way . . . This is a remarkable, well-balanced account of a "grand historical subject" and "must" for anyone interested in the period'   *Historical Novels Review*

'A valuable series of reflections on religious reform and related events which will interest the general reader; it is in no sense a textbook'   Paul Johnson, *Literary Review*

'A superb account . . . the book is loaded with gems of observation'   *Evangelical Times*

'Collinson gives us the profound insights of a distinguished career of teaching religious history . . . As a master storyteller, he certainly succeeds in providing a concise, elegant tour through key events, but its purpose runs deeper. He seeks to recapture the story of the Reformation; to see if "Humpty Dumpty can be put together again" after the autopsy . . . The reader, whether beginner or old hand, will find in this book some of the most incisive and illuminating articulations of central ideas that in their elegance almost mock decades of turgid Luther scholarship' *Times Higher Education Supplement*

Patrick Collinson read History at Cambridge before undertaking postgraduate research in London. After lectureships in Khartoum and King's College London, he held professorial chairs in Sydney, Kent at Canterbury, Sheffield and Cambridge, where he was Regius Professor of Modern History from 1988 to 1996. He is a Fellow of Trinity College, Cambridge. His books include *The Elizabethan Puritan Movement, The Religion of Portestants: The Church in English Society 1559–1625, Elizabethan Essays* and (as editor) *The Short Oxford History of the British Isles: the Sixteenth Century.* He delivered the Ford Lectures in Oxford in 1979, the Birkbeck Lectures in Cambridge in 1981 and the Creighton Lecture in London in 2002. He is a Fellow of the British Academy and of the Australian Academy of the Humanities, and holds the CBE. He lives in Derbyshire and Cambridge.

This book is dedicated to the memory of
GEORGE YULE,
Son and interpreter of the Reformation
and dear friend.

Contents

Preface

Between 1961 and 1975, I taught the history of the Reformation, first at King's College, London, and then at the University of Sydney. In Sydney I delivered more than twenty lectures every year on Martin Luther and related topics. When I added some lectures on the English Reformation, my more perceptive students said, 'Here is a subject you actually know something about.' In the pages that follow it will be hard to conceal from the intelligent reader my love of Luther, and some knowledge of England. Later, at the universities of Kent at Canterbury, Sheffield and Cambridge, such expertise as I commanded in the history of the Reformation on the Continent became almost redundant. There were accredited European historians to look after the subject and I was reduced to two annual lectures on Luther – in Cambridge, none. In Canterbury there was Gerhard Benecke, in Sheffield Mark Greengrass, in Cambridge Bob Scribner, the latchets of whose shoes I am not worthy to stoop down and unloose (Mark 1:7).

Bob is no longer here, which is still hard to accept. I want Lois to know that he was looking over my shoulder, I hope not breathing down my neck, as I wrote. We also mourn Heiko Oberman, a great historian of the Reformation and a good man, whose company I shared in Arizona in March 2001 in the very last days of his life, even as I began to think about this little book. Other influences, more implicit than explicit, have been Margaret Aston, John Bossy, Diarmaid MacCulloch, Eamon

Duffy, Keith Thomas, and that warm-hearted and wonderful Australian, George Yule, a dear friend who also departed in 2001, and to whose memory this book is dedicated.

I have never ceased to be interested in the big picture of the Reformation, regretting the provincialism and insularity of English students of the subject (including myself). This little book is a way of paying my respects to a grand historical subject. I hope that those who really know about the Reformation and who have never had to cut corners will not regard it as an insult. Try covering the Reformation, the whole thing, in little more than fifty thousand words! It owes more than I can say to my students on four continents, especially, thinking of those Australian years, the brothers John and Robert Gascoigne. Nor do I forget A. G. Dickens, my colleague at King's in the sixties and yet another great Reformation scholar to have died, full of years, in 2001. What a privilege it was to have taught alongside him!

Few of the usual acknowledgements to the helpfulness of archivists and librarians are called for. They have had little to do with this book, which has come out of my head and off my own shelves. Whatever was not there is not here. In this book I have let my hair down and have probably made mistakes too numerous to count. Old men forget. And much will appear dated to those still active at the coalface. My main responsibility has been to the general reader who may know very little about the Reformation, and I have tried my best to make issues that are remote from today's thinking and concerns as accessible as possible. Better to be wrong than to be boring, I always say, but to be neither is best, as several of those named here could have shown me. I am grateful to Eamon Duffy and Mark Greengrass, who read some of the chapters and offered their helpful criticism. Thanks to Eamon, I no longer refer to Luther's performance at the Colloquy of Leipizig as having happened in the 'hot dog days' of 1519. In spite of his verbal diarrhoea, there is much that we do not know about Martin Luther, including what may have been his taste in mustard.

Trinity College, Cambridge
5 November 2002
Remember! remember!

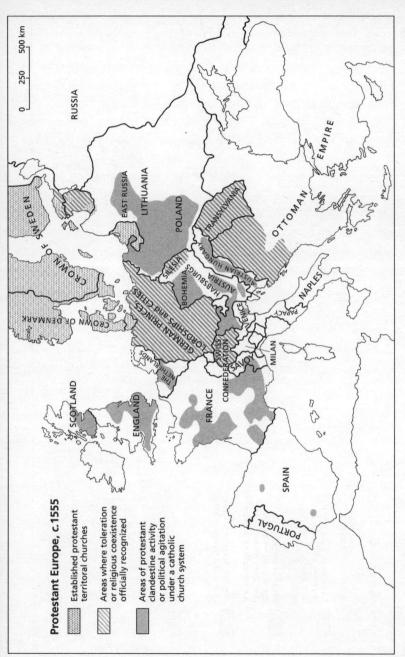

Protestant Europe, c.1555

Established protestant territorial churches

Areas where toleration or religious coexistence officially recognized

Areas of protestant clandestine activity or political agitation under a catholic church system

These maps are reprinted from *The European Reformation* by Euan Cameron, by permission of Oxford University Press.
© 1991 Euan Cameron.

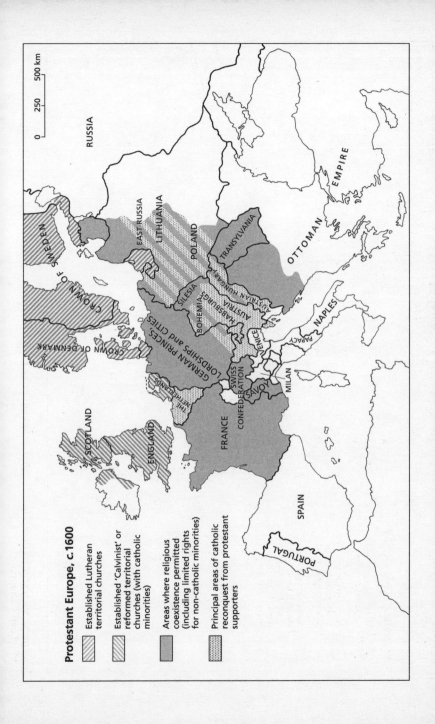

Protestant Europe, c.1600

Established Lutheran territorial churches

Established 'Calvinist' or reformed territorial churches (with catholic minorities)

Areas where religious coexistence permitted (including limited rights for non-catholic minorities)

Principal areas of catholic reconquest from protestant supporters

0   250   500 km

RUSSIA

CROWN OF SWEDEN

CROWN OF DENMARK

EAST RUSSIA

LITHUANIA

POLAND

TRANSYLVANIA

SILESIA

BOHEMIA

HABSBURG

AUSTRIA

AUSTRIAN HUNGARY

OTTOMAN EMPIRE

GERMAN PRINCES, LORDSHIPS and CITIES

THE NETHERLANDS

SCOTLAND

ENGLAND

FRANCE

SWISS CONFEDERATION

SAVOY

MILAN

VENICE

PAPACY

NAPLES

SPAIN

PORTUGAL

I *Reformation, what Reformation?*

This is a book about the Christian West: Western Christendom, almost equivalent to what would become 'Europe', the Europe of the EU before enlargement but minus Greece. The Western Church, whether obedient or disobedient to that self-appointed successor of St Peter, the bishop of Rome, has never paid much attention to Eastern Christendom, from which it parted company a millennium ago. Whether Western Christendom is entitled to think as much of itself as it always has done, not least in investing with a kind of cosmic significance certain events in its history in the sixteenth and seventeenth centuries, is one of the questions lurking in the background of our investigation of the Reformation.

By comparison with the West, Eastern Christendom is not monolithic but rather a family of Churches. Besides those claiming the title 'Orthodox' and acknowledging the honorary primacy of the patriarch of Constantinople as 'Oecumenical', there were and are other ancient Churches defined both ethnically and by ancient, half-forgotten, but apparently unbridgeable dogmatic differences. They include the Armenians, whose king embraced Christianity and made it the official religion of his kingdom early in the fourth century, a little before Constantine did the same thing for the Roman Empire. Another is the Coptic Church of Egypt, which went its own way doctrinally after the Council of Chalcedon (AD 451) defined 'Orthodoxy', insisting that Christ had only one nature

('Monophysitism') and not the Orthodox two, a breach that has so far lasted for fifteen hundred years. Its daughter Church in Ethiopia, which since 1959 has called itself the Ethiopian Orthodox Church, is something else, although until 1959 it received its one and only bishop from the Coptic patriarchate of Alexandria. Inseparably identified with the Ethiopian nation, its worship is conducted in an early form of the national languages of that country, and it retains many Jewish features which are perhaps fossils of early Christian practice, such as observance of the Jewish Sabbath and abstention from the forbidden meats of the Old Testament.

Although enough has happened to make it possible, and an interesting exercise, to write the histories of any or all of these Churches, those histories have been relatively lacking in evolutionary, let alone revolutionary, transformations. None of the Eastern Churches has experienced anything like the Reformation and its reactive Counter-Reformation, although the schism of the Old Believers in Russia (from 1667 until the present day) may be the exception to prove this rule.

However, in all these manifestations of the Christian faith – as, indeed, in religion more generally and globally – we find the eternal principles of renewal and conversion. The Christian baptism of infants, which has in effect been compulsory wherever the religion has remained publicly and politically established, may suggest that the Church is something into which people are born. Yet it is individuals in their uniqueness who are baptized, and every child, through sponsors or 'godparents', has to renounce the Devil and all his works and turn personally to Christ. For baptism is, or ought to be, that second birth that Jesus explained to the Jewish elder Nicodemus: 'Ye must be born again.' In Ethiopia, there is an annual ceremony in which the 'tabot', a replica of the Jewish Ark of the Covenant, containing the altar stones, is carried with much ceremony from each church to the nearest water, into which the people plunge in order to renew their baptism. This is the time known as 'Maskal' (which means the Cross) when the Ethiopian spring bursts out after the great rains, bright with yellow maskal daisies. The symbolism is obvious. In present-day Anglican churches, when a child is baptized the practice is to invite the whole congregation to repeat and renew their own baptismal vows. This can happen, too, at the European spring festival of Easter, another season of renewal.

In these examples, the principle of renewal is, to use an ugly sociological term, routinized. What is supposed to be an event becomes a time-out-of-mind custom and an institution: continuity rather than discontinuity. But the flow of religious history has always been punctuated and diverted by episodes and experiences of conversion. In the Judaeo-Christian story, Abram was told by God, 'Get thee out of thy country, and from thy kindred,' and even his name was changed, to Abraham. Moses was called by God out of a burning bush to give up his occupation as a shepherd and to lead his people out of Egyptian slavery. The prophet Isaiah had a vision of the Lord of Hosts who said, '"Whom shall I send, and who will go for us?" Then said I, "Here am I; send me."' John the Baptist summoned the people of his time to repentance in a setting full of symbolism, the Judaean desert, through which flowed the River Jordan. Jesus told a tale about the repentance of the prodigal son who, when in utter dereliction, 'came to himself' and returned to his father. Saul of Tarsus was on his way to persecute the early Christians when he was blinded by a light from heaven, the 'Damascus road experience'. This was his call to be an Apostle, and Paul (for he, too, changed his name) went on, in the opinion of many, to invent and construct Christianity itself.

This at least superficially repetitive factor recurs throughout the history of Christianity. The conversion of St Augustine, thanks to his *Confessions*, became a paradigm consciously or unconsciously imitated and replicated. Francis of Assisi renounced all worldly goods and the very clothes he stood up in in order to reinvent the *vita apostolica*. Ignatius Loyola, a soldier recovering from his wounds, was converted by reading religious books (there being nothing else to read) and this was followed by a series of intense religious experiences out of which the Society of Jesus was born. What if he had been killed in that battle, or had found some novels to read? John Wesley's 'heart was strangely warmed' on 24 May 1738 (moments of conversion are supposed to be that precise) when he heard Martin Luther's Preface to St Paul's Epistle to the Romans read in a chapel in Aldersgate Street in London. The consequence of that event was the thick strand of Protestant Christianity known as Methodism. Without Methodism, Élie Halévy thought that there might have been an English Revolution along the lines of 1789. England had a religious revolution instead, which bred self-help, trade unionism and a non-revolutionary but sturdy popular politics.

It is, of course, that same Luther with whom everyone must engage who attempts to write a history of the Reformation. For without Luther, we can be reasonably certain that there would have been no Reformation, or not the same Reformation. Thomas Carlyle went further. His history was the story of heroic individuals, and he thought that if Luther had not stuck to his guns at the Diet of Worms, where he stood before the Holy Roman emperor and refused to recant ('Here I stand'), there would have been no French Revolution and no America:

the principle that inspired those cataclysmic events would have been killed in the womb. No one would now make such a claim. But we can still ask the question: was the Reformation, or was it not, a kind of midwife to the modern world?

Luther told on more than one occasion the story of his own conversion. The different accounts are not entirely consistent with each other or with what we otherwise know about his life and career around the time it is supposed to have happened, when he was in his early thirties and a professor of theology in one of the new German universities. We know that the experience arose from a strenuous engagement with the theology of Paul to the Romans: the sufficiently technical, but for Luther thoroughly existential, problem of how *justitia Dei*, the punitive righteousness of God, was to be satisfied. Luther knew that Christ had already made satisfaction, as Christians had always affirmed, 'for the sins of the whole world'. But how was that satisfaction to be applied to the individual Christian believer? Only, Luther discovered, by faith in Christ's sacrifice. Human moral striving was actually counterproductive, turning the soul ever more in upon itself. That was as much as to say that God, who is merciful, makes us righteous by a faith that God himself works in us. This has been called a kind of Copernican revolution in thinking about God. God, not man, is the centre and prime mover of all things, including human salvation. Theologically, that had never been in doubt. In practice, however, the system of medieval Christianity emphasized moral effort, in effect a journey towards a God who, Luther insisted, is actually reaching out to us. According to other references to this moment that Luther made from time to time around the dinner table, it happened in a tower where he had his professorial study in the monastic house of the

Augustinian canons, Luther's religious order: the so-called *Turmerlebnis*, or 'tower experience'.

According to Luther, this was indeed an experience, not simply an intellectual process: 'I felt myself straightway born afresh and to have entered through the open gates into paradise itself.' But that was only the beginning, and he went on to explain that he told the story, 'as Augustine said of himself', so that it should not be thought that he 'had suddenly from nothing become supreme', or 'with one glance at scripture exhausted the total spirit of its contents'. Indeed, Luther did not come from nothing but out of the rich resources of late medieval theology.

We may be still more cautious about Luther's sudden *Durchbruch* (breakthrough) if we consider what happened at about the same time to an Englishman, the Cambridge scholar Thomas Bilney, who had probably never heard of Luther. Reading, in the elegant Latin of a new translation of the New Testament by Erasmus, the words that 'Christ Jesus came into the world to save sinners,' Bilney tells us, 'immediately I felt a marvellous comfort and quietness, insomuch that my bruised bones leaped for joy.' That was the beginning of the Protestant Reformation in Cambridge, which led the way in all of England and, after that, North America.

There is a tension here between event and process which, projected onto a larger screen, is the tension between the Reformation as part of the continuum of history and the Reformation as an extraordinary historical moment – as it were, a meteor strike at history. For Max Weber such interruptions in history represented the operations of what he called 'charisma', something that, as a social scientist, he did not presume to explain. Such figures as Moses, or Isaiah, or Luther, were 'charismatic'.

What happened to these deeply religious Catholics and children of the later Middle Ages was no doubt compressed in their imaginative recollections into an almost conventional scenario, biblical and Augustinian, of blinding revelation and a total overturning of what they had always believed and taken for granted. In Jesus's words, they had indeed been born again. The historian who wants to measure the watershed separating the medieval world from what overtook and overturned it must take seriously the perception that those living through these events had of an almost total transformation. Another Englishman expressed the wish that God would bless an elderly uncle, 'and make him now to know which in his tender years he could not see, for the world was then dark, and we were blind in it'. For him, the Catholic Church was not merely defective but actually antichristian, its pope Antichrist himself, the great deceiver. So the landscapes of both time and space were subject to a radical and seismic reconstruction, and a series of aftershocks would be experienced for a century and more to come.

Whole communities, Churches and states shared in both the initial upheaval and the aftershocks. As Luther's theology was systematized as Lutheranism, large areas of Germany, which is to say the governments of princes and cities on behalf of their subjects, formally adopted what became known as the Evangelical confession. Other governments promoted a variant form of Protestantism, more thorough in its departure from traditional Catholicism and developed in the cities and cantons of southwest Germany and Switzerland, above all in Geneva where John Calvin was intellectually and spiritually dominant. These were the Reformed Churches, the title indicating their claim to be the 'best reformed'. Faithful to the principle of *cuius regio, eius religio*, the principle that the ruler determines the religion of his state, the Rhenish Palatinate in south-west Germany was successively Evangelical, Reformed, briefly Evangelical again, Reformed, and ultimately somewhat brutally re-Catholicized. The principle was defied in France, where a sizeable Protestant (and Reformed) minority enjoyed strong political and military support, which plunged the country into decades of (partly) religious war. In the Netherlands it was turned on its head, religion sustaining a revolt against the legitimate government of Spain and helping to give birth to a new kind of politics, that of the independent republic. England, which at the beginning of the sixteenth century seems to have been one of the most Catholic countries in Europe, became, by the seventeenth century, the most virulently anti-Catholic, and the almost dominant ideology of anti-Catholicism fuelled the civil wars that engulfed all parts of the British Isles in mid-century and later provoked the Bloodless Revolution from which what passes for a British constitution derives.

This, however, is not where the inquiry should end. Nobody doubts that the sixteenth and seventeenth centuries were a time of change, confusion and conflict for countless individuals, local communities, and whole states and nations. It is not wrong to call this an era of religious wars, comparable in scale to the revolutionary, nationalistic and ideological wars of the subsequent centuries. The only question is whether these circumstances were so different from the experience of earlier and later centuries as to make this a major turning point in European civilization, at least as important as, if not more so than, the Scientific Revolution, the Enlightenment of the eighteenth century, or the Age of Revolutions which began in 1776 and 1789. Making some of those comparisons, a distinguished historian of the last generation, Sir Herbert Butterfield, called both the Reformation and the Renaissance, which was its necessary precondition, merely internal displacements in European history. Others have doubted whether the Reformation represented any kind of radical departure from the mentalities, politics or social structures of medieval Europe, or had anything to do with the shaping of the modern world. We may now find it helpful to speak of the medieval Church and *its* Reformation. Martin Luther, a medieval rather than a modern man, offered new answers to old questions. He asked no new ones.

A receding view alters in perspective, mountains no longer tower, and sharp and bold outlines are softened and blurred. It has become fashionable to demote the Reformation to lower case and to pluralize it: many reformations, both before and since what was once regarded as *the* Reformation, and in other places and other cultures. A recent textbook puts the Reformation into global perspective, placing this European event alongside the revival of the Confucian philosophy in China after a thousand years by the brothers Ch'eng-i and Ch'eng-hao (in the late eleventh century AD), or with the reconstruction of Islam by Muhammad ibn 'Abd-al-Wahhab (1703–91 AD) which, as Wahhabite Islam, became the state religion of Saudi Arabia. Another author, Felipe Fernández-Armesto, sticking to Christian parallels, makes 'reformation' a principle of world religion from 1500 to 2000, not a decisive, divisive event but 'a continuing story, embracing the common religious experiences of Christians of different traditions worldwide'. He takes us to the shores of a lake in Guatemala, the scene of a rich mixture of religions, Catholic, evangelical and syncretist, to ecstatic religious dancers in Zaire (now the Democratic Republic of the Congo), the mass weddings of Moonies in Korea, 'behatted Scottish lady Presbyterians', a Catholic priest in New Guinea celebrating mass in a grass skirt, and to a crematorium in a London suburb where a family who never go to church are led through the motions by a stranger, a vicar with a drink problem. All of these are not only part of religion's rich tapestry but manifestations of 'reformation' in its myriad shapes and forms. That may be fun but it is not very helpful.

More responsibly, and surveying only the English Reformation scene, another historian proposes a plurality of successive reformations, treating what happened in the sixteenth century as equivalent on the Richter scale to later changes of religious fashion such as evangelicalism in the eighteenth century or High Church neo-Catholicism in the nineteenth. Other historians of English religion speak of a 'Long Reformation', reverberating for centuries. All of these events constituted what the nineteenth century learned to call 'revivals', or perhaps a continuity containing within itself the constant expectation of revival. However, it may be a serious distortion of history to diminish the critical beginnings of this lengthy process, in which any historian of *the* Reformation is bound still to believe.

Meanwhile, the French historian Jean Delumeau has argued that what the Protestant Reformation and the Catholic Counter-Reformation had in common was more important than what divided them. Both were episodes of almost primary Christianization in which the rural populations of Europe were confronted for the first time with what it meant to be a Christian, a process of profound internalization. The Ten Commandments were common ground, and were almost newly discovered ground in their implications for individual conduct and conscience. However, John Bossy, an English historian with a cosmopolitan European outlook, doubts that. The West was Christian before 1500 and it is absurd to suggest otherwise, although it is true, he thinks, that it was then that the Commandments took over from the Seven Deadly Sins as the new moral gold standard.

As a historian exceptionally sensitive to terminology, Bossy is tempted to get rid of the Reformation altogether. As a word, rather than a thing, it may be a hindrance rather than a help to understanding what was going on with regard to religion in Europe within the scope of his book *Christianity in the West 1400–1700*. The index has only three entries under 'Reformation', the first subheaded 'term discussed'. That something important happened in the sixteenth century Bossy does not doubt, 'and the term "Reformation" is probably as good a guide as any to investigating what it was'. But it is to be used as sparingly as possible, 'not simply because it goes along too easily with the notion that a bad form of Christianity was being replaced by a good one, but because it sits awkwardly across the subject without directing one's attention anywhere in particular'; it is 'too high-flown to cope with actual social behaviour, and not high-flown enough to deal sensitively with thought, feeling, or culture'.

It might be thought that the Humpty-Dumpty of the Reformation has by now fallen off its wall and that the aim of what follows will be to see whether we should, or can, put Humpty together again. But all those other reformations are only called 'reformations' because of their supposed relation and resemblance to elements of *the* Reformation. Without *the* Reformation the word would never have been used for what happened in the tenth century, or the twelfth century, or the eighteenth century, or for what some of our deconstructionists suggest is always happening.

So perhaps we can manage without all the king's horses and all the king's men. In 1991 a 564-page book on *The European Reformation* was published; 1996 saw the launch of the four-volume, 1977-page *Oxford Encyclopedia of the Reformation*; 1999 heralded a substantial book called *Europe's Reformations*;

in 2000, 576 pages appeared on *The Reformation World*; and in 2001 the greatest living English historian of the Christian Church, Owen Chadwick, published *The Early Reformation on the Continent*. In 2004 Routledge brought out a 4-volume collection of 72 articles on *The Reformation*; selling at €475. It is not, after all, so easy to change the terminological and periodical structures within which we historians operate, although they must not be allowed to become watertight boxes in which we cease to think.

2   The late medieval Church and its Reformation

No revolution however drastic has ever involved a total repudiation of what came before it. What do revolutionaries have to work with but the ideas and aspirations that they have inherited? What was Stalin but a new kind of tsar? Thomas Hobbes pronounced that 'the Papacy is not other than the Ghost of the deceased Roman Empire, sitting crowned upon the grave thereof'. Jesus was not the first Christian, and Luther was not a Lutheran.

Luther denounced much of the religious practice of his day in a rising crescendo of protest which soon left very little of the old Church intact. He defined the Church in grossly reductionist terms, simply as the sheep who hear their shepherd's whistle: 'A child seven years old knows what the Church is, namely the holy believers and the lambs that hear the shepherd's voice.' For Leo X, the pope who excommunicated him, here was a wild boar, rooting up the carefully tended vineyard of the Church. Luther responded by calling the pope 'the man of sin and son of perdition', 'the end and dregs of all ages', and, towards the end of his life, in a book that he admitted had not 'pleased everyone equally', 'Most Hellish Father'.

The paradox is that Luther's criticism came from deep within the very tradition that he denounced. It is a serious mistake, Carlyle's mistake, to suppose that at the Diet of Worms Luther was claiming the sovereignty of his own conscience, as if the fact that he believed something to be true made it true, at least for him – what Wilhelm Dilthey called 'the autocracy of the believing person'. That would have been a modern state of mind and Luther was not a modern man. Luther's conscience, every conscience, was enthralled by the Bible as the Word of God, the only true foundation of the faith of the Church. It is the beginning of wisdom to understand that the Reformation was not, in its own eyes, a novelty. The novelties were those grave distortions of the truth that had passed for truth in more recent centuries, and which we know as medieval Catholicism. Yet Luther was himself some kind of late medieval Catholic. And even to say harsh things about the supreme pontiff was itself part of the late medieval legacy.

'Reform' was a somewhat shop-soiled mantra long before the Reformation. 'Reformation' (another way of translating the Latin *reformatio*) was a distinctly different and rather more concrete formulation which, however, not even the sixteenth century invested with all the portmanteau meaning it would later have for historians. In the eleventh century Pope Gregory had presided over what history knows as the Gregorian reforms, designed to rescue the Church from the corrupting influence of secularization by insisting on clerical celibacy and an end to the buying and selling of church offices ('simony') and lay control of the Church's affairs. In 1215 another reforming pope, Innocent III, convened in Rome the fourth of the Church Councils held in the Lateran Palace, which formulated what was to become the official doctrine of the Eucharist and required all Christians to make an annual confession of their sins, a considerable landmark.

Pope Innocent and the Fourth Lateran Council also thought it a desirable reform to prevent the formation of new religious orders, so that the Franciscan and Dominican friars were the last under the wire, both of them expressions of the vigorous reforming impulses of their founders, St Francis and St Dominic. The early Franciscans, for whom the unworldly rule of complete poverty was always problematical, having split between a minority of hardliners, the so-called Spirituals, and the more conventional majority, later experienced a further rupture which divided a new generation of strict Observants from the more lax Conventuals. One of many 'reforms' in the early years of the sixteenth century itself was the regularization of a new, reformed Franciscan breakaway order, the Capuchins, who went back to wearing the rough cloak of Francis, tied with a simple cord, and sandals. Almost every religious order in the fifteenth and early sixteenth centuries had its own 'observant' (we might say 'fundamentalist') tendencies, including Luther's own order, the Augustinian canons.

The world into which Martin Luther was born in 1483 was full of new religious things. There were new theological and intellectual fashions, which included a reappropriation of St Thomas Aquinas among the Dominicans, and a revived interest in St Augustine and St Paul, critical influences on Luther's own mind. There were newly rediscovered saints such as Mary Magdalene, a conflation of Mary the sister of Martha and Lazarus and the woman of easy virtue who washed Jesus's feet, who provided a model for the reform that required personal repentance for sin, as well as a way of addressing the 'woman question'. There was a new, or almost new, devotion to St Anne, mother of the Virgin Mary, who was popular among miners and metalworkers, and to whom the young Luther prayed when caught out in a violent thunderstorm, 'St Anne help me! I will become a monk,' his first conversion. The Virgin herself had never been so popular, the Virgins of this and that place vying for the custom of pilgrims – in England, Our Lady of

Willesden versus Our Lady of Ipswich. At Regensburg in south-east Germany, where a synagogue was being demolished to make way for a church (anti-Semitism was never far away), there was an industrial accident and a miraculous cure wrought by (who else?) the Virgin. In 1520 twelve thousand souvenir tokens were sold to pilgrims to 'our lovely lady' of Regensburg, some of whom are shown in a contemporary woodcut lying around her image in various states of ecstatic collapse (or inebriation?).

Objects and centres of devotion of this kind were rarely planned and constructed by those who claimed to be in charge of the Church. Typically they arose from popular 'devotion', often uncontrolled. Everywhere the church authorities were engaged in delicate balancing acts. Should they encourage or discourage such spontaneity? In late fourteenth-century Lincolnshire somebody (or perhaps a small syndicate) put up a wooden cross in a field and began to adore it and to report miracles. 'They are preaching and ringing bells and holding processions, for the deception of the people and the increase of gain, and laymen are said to be converting the offerings to their own uses.' The bishop decided that this was a holy racket and ordered the suppression of the instant cult. Six years later, however, the pope, presumably in response to lobbying, licensed the building of a chapel close to the miracle-working cross, which was now claimed to be a hundred years old. That the late medieval Church condoned so many practices that were over the fine line separating 'religion' from 'superstition' suggests that it was already familiar with the popular adage that if you can't beat them you might as well join them.

What might seem to us to have been higher and more debased forms of devotion could be coexistent within the same individual. The elector of Saxony, Frederick the Wise, Luther's prince, was at one and the same time the patron of a modern university with a progressive faculty of theology and the proud owner of one of the largest collections in the world of sacred relics, which were held to have the power to reduce the time spent in purgatory by many thousands of years. The new technology of printing with movable type was employed to publish a catalogue of his collection.

Modern Christians may find it easier to identify with reform in the shape of the intense Christocentrism of the early sixteenth century, and to recognize this as something that nourished the religion of the reformer Martin Luther. In England, the cult of the Holy Name of Jesus was popular and many of the churches built or reconstructed in this period are studded with the monogrammatic emblem of the Holy Name, IHS. Both before and after the Reformation it was thought to be the business of preachers to 'preach Christ'. In Alsace, Matthias Grünewald painted a triptych for a convent south of Colmar, now the museum of Unterdenlinden, which has at its centre a crucified Christ so tortured that it is hard to look upon it without emotion. Albrecht Dürer not only depicted a poignantly suffering Christ in his two woodcut series of the Passion but in more than one self-portrait iconographically identified himself with the Man of Sorrows. Just as Christ on the cross uttered the words of one of the most sombre of the Psalms ('My God, my God, why hast thou forsaken me?'), so Luther, lecturing on the Psalms, invited participation in the experience of the suffering Christ: 'As in Christ, so let it be in me.'

Mysticism was a constant source of renewal, especially in the fourteenth century, its more notable English practitioners including the woman called Julian of Norwich, her contemporary the unknown author of the treatise called *The Cloud of Unknowing*, and a whole succession of writers in the north of

England who left behind the spiritual equivalents of modern cook-books. Although Luther was later suspicious of speculative mysticism as a kind of shortcut and man-made ladder to heaven, his earliest published work (the first of many hundreds) was an edition of the anonymous *Theologia Germanica* (which he called *Deutsch Theologia*), a work that expressed the religion of the people who called themselves Friends of God, followers of a succession of spiritual teachers including Meister Eckhart and his disciple Johannes Tauler. Tauler's emphasis on suffering (*Leiden*) was in the same key signature as Luther's early theology.

Reform in the fifteenth-century Netherlands and the neighbouring Rhineland took the shape of a religious movement called the New Devotion practised by a semi-monastic brotherhood, the Brethren of the Common Life. This was to have a profound impact on higher education in the sixteenth century, by which time the spiritual creativity of the Devotion had succumbed to a rancid and repressive puritanism, to which Erasmus, Calvin and Rabelais were all in their turn subjected by the Christian Brothers of the sixteenth century.

The New Devotion had begun, however, as a modified, adapted method of mystical devotion, which sought to rescue mysticism from the dangers of pantheism and elitism to which it was always prone and to make it a valuable resource for the Church at large. When everything else about this episode in Christian history is forgotten, the world may remember one of its products, a little book called *The Imitation of Christ* (1418), traditionally but dubiously ascribed to a certain Thomas à Kempis. A succession of English versions by translators from both sides of the growing confessional divide was published in 1504, 1531, 1567, 1580, 1613 and 1636, and later by John Wesley and in the twentieth century by Monsignor Ronald Knox.

All this may suggest that at the most authentic level of spirituality, contemplation and prayer, the Reformation was a mere hiccup and the continuities were stronger than the discontinuities. The literature of the New Devotion helped to convert the Basque soldier Ignatius Loyola and fed into his *Spiritual Exercises*, which in turn inspired the *Christian directorie*, or *Booke of the christian exercise*, published in the late sixteenth century by the English Jesuit Robert Parsons. Parsons' book was immediately turned by English Protestants into a bowdlerized version, which went through many more editions than the original: seventeen in the first year, fifteen more up to 1638. Here was an admission that English Protestantism, even in the years of its most rabid anti-Catholicism, still craved the spiritual resources of the old Church.

'Reform' was on everyone's lips in the fifteenth century – the equivalent, as it were, of 'motherhood and apple pie'. The word is often encountered in the formulation 'reform of the Church in head and members', and at this level the object of reform was supposed to be the whole body of the Church but more especially its very highest echelons. That the Church was in need of searching, excoriating reform was underlined by the scandal of the Great Schism, when for a whole generation (1378–1417) it was divided in its obedience between two or, for a time, three different popes. For seventy years prior to this the papacy had been located not at Rome but at Avignon and was under predominantly French influence. The luxury of Avignon, which tourists to the Palais des Papes can still inspect, was denounced by the poet Petrarch and others as a 'Babylonian captivity'. The last Avignonese pope, Gregory XI, who was French, had returned to Rome, persuaded by the pleas of a saint, Catherine of Siena, who addressed him as '*dulcissimo babbo mio*' (my sweetest daddy). Rome now tried to regain the papacy for itself, but the election, under duresss from a mob, of an Italian, Urban VI, provoked the counter-election of a Frenchman, Clement VII, who returned to Avignon. Obediences were divided along the political frontiers of Europe. Since France was for Clement, England naturally supported Urban, which meant that Scotland was for Clement. The situation was full of practical inconveniences. How could anyone be sure of the validity of any of the judgements and administrative acts that determined the distribution of property and offices? But the deeper scandal was ideological, exposing the implausibility of the claim of the bishop of Rome to be St Peter's successor and Christ's vicar on earth.

Some already realized that the logic of this impasse was that each kingdom should have its own pope. In a series of settlements that eventually resolved the crisis, concordats were made with the secular powers that gave them many of the advantages in respect of resources and appointments that Henry VIII of England was to seize for himself unilaterally in the 1530s. The writing was already on the wall for the kind of papacy that Gregory VII and Innocent III had created. In the long term, through the sixteenth-century process known as the Counter-Reformation, later popes would find the solution to their problem by creating a new kind of Church, one more separate than it had been from the secular monarchies, while they themselves became secular monarchs of a medium-sized Italian principality. (Between 1523 and 1978 there were no non-Italian popes.) In their spiritual domain of a state without frontiers and (as Stalin said) with few battalions, they could hope to enjoy something approaching the same absolute power to which the secular monarchies aspired. This centralized spiritual state was destined to last until the Second Vatican

Council of the 1960s, and in some respects is still with us in the pontificate of John Paul II.

But that is to jump ahead. While the Great Schism remained unresolved, there were idealists and intellectuals who understood its deeper causes and saw an opportunity to reconstruct the Church along very different and, as we might say, constitutional lines. Ever since the political philosophy of Aristotle had been reappropriated in the mid-thirteenth century it had been possible to think of political societies, the Church included, as constituted of their various parts, not simply as expressions of the will of the ruler. This sort of thinking had affected even those legal circles in which arguments had been developed to support the claim of the pope to *plenitudo potestatis*, a plenitude of power, almost to *be* the Church. But what if the pope were to be insane (which those who deserted Urban VI in 1378 suspected on good grounds to be the case) or otherwise incapacitated?

What, moreover, if it proved impossible, with the best will in the world, to determine who was pope? History had seen many antipopes but it was always reasonably clear that that is what they were. This was different. Intellectuals, especially the Parisian intellectuals of the day, came to believe that only a General Council, taking precedence over anyone claiming to be pope, could restore unity; hence they became known as 'conciliarists', with a coherent ideology of 'conciliarism'. But who could call such a Council but the legitimate pope? Against all tradition, a General Council was called at Pisa in 1409 on the authority of some of the cardinals of both obediences and in defiance of the two rival popes, now Benedict XIII and Gregory XII. However, Pisa succeeded only in compounding the Schism by adding a third pope, Alexander V, whom both Benedict and Gregory naturally repudiated.

When Alexander's successor, John XXIII (not to be confused with the pope who took that name in 1958), was persuaded to summon the Council that met at Constance in 1414, the conciliarists knew that only truly radical remedies would work. The Council enacted a decree, *Haec Sancta*, that declared in effect that the whole is greater than its parts, even that part which was the head of the body, the pope. The Council held its power from Christ directly, and everyone, 'of whatever condition rank or dignity, including the pope', was bound to obey it in any measures taken to end the Schism and to reform the Church 'in its head and in its members'.

A further decree, *Frequens*, was intended to place the government of the Church on a permanently conciliar footing by requiring Councils to be held at regular intervals. However, once the Council of Constance had decided to heal the Schism before considering wider programmes of reform, had got rid of all three popes, including John XXIII who had summoned it, and had elected a new pope, Martin V, whom everyone acknowledged, such radical conciliarism had an uncertain future. Another Council duly met at Basle in 1431, but it soon set itself against Pope Eugenius IV and a long endgame was played out. Basle lasted eighteen years, but it went down in confusion when in 1439 it elected its own antipope.

These events had the fateful consequence of making papalism and conciliarism into opposed ideologies for a full century to come. When all was said and done, the pope was the pope, commanding the well-oiled machine of the Curia, and the Council was so much hot air. In future, though, monarchs would play the conciliar card in their own interests, as when the French king Louis XII staged a nakedly antipapal Council at Pisa to which Pope Julius II responded by convoking the Fifth Lateran Council (1512–17). This is why the papacy took so long to respond to Luther's Reformation. By the time the Council of Trent met in 1545 the only answer that Catholicism could give to Protestantism was to define itself as its negative image, not to heal the breach.

The reader whose hobby is not collecting the names of fifteenth-century popes may deserve an apology. But there is a good reason for having told this story in some detail. The question we have to confront is whether the conciliarism of Constance and Basle could have pre-empted the Reformation, making such a violent rupture, far more damaging than the Great Schism, unnecessary. It is a little like bringing the so-called Bloodless Revolution of 1688 in England to bear on the French Revolution: if France had had a 1688, could it have saved itself 1789?

History is unable to answer questions of this kind, since the past is not a game that can be replayed with the pieces on the board changed or rearranged. What we can say is that 'reform in head and members' was a good slogan but never much more. Reform was always on the agenda at every ecclesiastical summit between 1378 and 1514, but little was ever achieved. The members saw the need to reform the head, and each other, for the members were in practice not so much interdependent parts of the body, as St Paul had idealized the Church (he wrote, 'the body is not one member . . . they are many members, yet but one body'), as sectional interests that tended to pull against each other, popes and secular rulers, bishops and their clergy, religious orders and universities. I do not need to be reformed. You do.

Only one thing was capable of uniting the various parties and interests that constituted the German Church: resentment of Rome. In about 1451 a German priest addressed the cardinal-legate to his country, the scholar and statesman Nicholas of

Cusa, himself a German: 'The Cardinal-Legate has come to us in order to reform our nation. But how shall he succeed in this reform? If the head is sick, the limbs also feel the pain. If reform is to be accomplished, it must begin with the pope and the Roman curia. It is the pope and the cardinals who daily commit the most fearful transgression and abuses . . .' Luther was not the first German to criticize the papacy, and when in 1520 he wrote *The Babylonian Captivity of the Church* and his *Address to the Christian Nobility of the German Nation* it was in a tradition of articulated grievances, the *Gravamina nationis Germanicae*, which was already almost a century old.

It was easy to blame all the Church's ills on Rome. The endless talk of reform that was the overture to the Reformation was in large part a fantasy dependent on a myth that once upon a time, in some golden age, the Church had been pure and in no need of reform. It had little connection with the real state of affairs or with what 'reform' could actually be expected to achieve. Indeed, many of the reforms proposed would probably have proved damaging rather than helpful.

Our last question, as we leave the years before the storm of the Reformation broke, is whether anyone, especially those on the bridge of the ship, ought to have seen it coming. Probably not, for Luther's challenge, although it found an instant response in those well-rehearsed and deeply felt German *Gravamina*, was different from anything that had gone before. He himself boasted that whereas others had concerned themselves merely with external abuses of the system, only he had attacked the corrupt theology of the Church in the name of what he claimed to be the true Christian Gospel and Word of God. Luther, who liked a pungent phrase, would have been glad to agree that only he had gone for the jugular. And here we can propose a nice paradox: whereas a century of talk about reform had been no more than that, mere words on paper, Luther's single-minded concentration on the Word brought about real and revolutionary change.

Prior to Luther the Church had not been greatly challenged doctrinally and heresy was a marginal rather than a major problem, something that lurked in the Alpine valleys inhabited by the primitive Christians known as Waldensians. The two exceptions to prove this rule were the kingdoms of England and Bohemia, where the dissenting ideas of the Oxford scholar John Wyclif (c.1330–84) put down roots that were not easily torn out. In some ways and in the hands of some of its interpreters, Wyclifism could be more radical than anything proposed by the mainstream sixteenth-century reformers, corrosive as it could be of sacraments and the visible Church. The leading authority on this subject, Anne Hudson, has written of *The Premature Reformation* and has toyed with her own counterfactual question: what if the Reformation had started one hundred and fifty years earlier?

In England, however, the Lancastrian kings stamped down hard on heresy and legislated to burn heretics, so that the Bible-reading followers of Wyclif, called Lollards, unlike the English Protestants who were in some respects their children and grandchildren, failed to remain a significant political force and survived only as a fugitive and secretive minority. It was different in the Czech lands of Bohemia, where the reformer Jan Hus turned a religious revival, with a programme partly native, partly Wycliffite, into a national crusade, provoking a new series of crusading wars in retaliation. Hus's reformation entailed the expulsion of the Germans from Prague and its university, which was how the University of Lepizig came to be founded, by academic refugees. The Council of Constance, which was the idea of the German Holy Roman emperor,

Sigismund, was called partly to deal with this Central European problem. Hus was lured to Constance under a safe pardon and burned. Later, the Council of Basle found a reason for its existence in its partly successful efforts to defuse the problem of Bohemia.

In so far as 'Bohemian' and 'heretic' became virtually synonymous, Germany itself was reasonably proof against heretical contamination. One of Luther's difficulties, as his protest gathered momentum, was how to counter the accusation that he was nothing but a Bohemian and a Hussite. It was an electrifying and important moment at the Disputation of Leipzig (1519), where his opponent Johann Eck had opportunistically accused him of being tarred with Hus's brush, when Luther returned to the fray after some reading over lunch to announce that, so far as he could see, some of the doctrines for which Hus had been condemned were Christian and Evangelical. We are all Hussites without knowing it, or at least we ought to be. This was as much as to say that not only popes but a General Council such as Constance could err.

3   *Words, language and books*

The Reformation was awash with words. The historian who tries to catch its essence finds his net breaking under the weight of words. Words flowed ceaselessly out of Martin Luther's mouth and from his pen: a book a fortnight for thirty years, nearly a hundred large volumes in the standard modern edition of his works, written with no system in mind, least of all one called 'Lutheranism', but simply as the occasion demanded. Luther was full of something called 'the Word', which was not at all the same thing as 'words'. Rather it was the Logos of the opening words of St John's Gospel, 'In the beginning was the Word,' restating Genesis 1, 'In the beginning God . . .' As the old world collapsed around him, Luther was forever protesting that it was not his doing. 'While I slept or drank Wittenberg beer . . . the Word so greatly weakened the papacy that never a Prince or Emperor inflicted such damage upon it. I did nothing. The Word did it all.'

The formulation 'Word of God', which among Protestants especially became a synonym for the Bible, made the elusive abstraction 'the Word' hard and fast, more concrete, anchoring it in biblical texts, which were given a new and absolute authority: *sola scriptura*. The Church was to be validated by the Bible, not the Bible by the Church. So the English reformer William Tyndale, who was the first to propagate an English version of the New Testament in print, told the reader: 'I supposed it very necessary to put you in remembrance of . . .

what these words mean: the Old Testament, the New Testament, the law, the gospel, Moses, Christ.' Words became as tablets of stone.

A favourite text for Protestants was: 'Faith cometh by hearing, and hearing by the word of God' (Romans 10:17) Many insisted that hearing the Word preached was the *only* means of salvation. Not even reading the Bible would work. Some doubted whether deaf people could be saved. There is an anecdote about Luther to the effect that when he was criticized for not preaching enough he said, 'We do that with our books,' and this has been used to make the point that the Reformation was, to quote one historian, a matter of 'salvation by print alone'. But it is doubtful that Luther could ever have said it. Even such a compulsive writer knew that evangelism meant preaching. John Calvin's many thousands of sermons preached in Geneva were just that, sermons, and it was with reluctance that he allowed them to be published.

Hearing or reading, it was the Word that counted. The Reformation prescribed a new precedence of ear over eye. In the Preface to his edition of the New Testament, Erasmus, the greatest wordsmith of his age, wrote: 'These writings bring you . . . the speaking, healing, dying, rising Christ himself, and thus they render him so fully present that you would see less if you gazed upon him with your very eyes' – a paradox, but one that perfectly expresses the Renaissance belief in the creative power of language and 'good letters'.

Erasmus expressed the hope that the New Testament would be translated into all languages and made accessible (choosing some extreme cases) to Scots and Irish, Turks and Saracens. 'I would that even the lowliest women read the Gospels and the Pauline Epistles.' His 'would that' contrasts with the stronger word that Tyndale used in arguing the toss with a conservative clergyman in his native Gloucestershire: 'If God spare my life, ere many years, I will cause a boy that driveth the plough shall know more of the scripture than thou dost.' This duly came to pass, if not for every ploughboy at least for some, and even for the odd ploughgirl. A woman in Suffolk called Alice Driver, one of John Foxe's martyrs, told her judges that she had never been brought up in a university but had 'driven the plough before my father many a time'. Yet she ran rings round the ecclesiastics in her knowledge of scripture. Even for a writer like Foxe a learned woman was almost a contradiction in terms, and he was using these cases to castigate a Catholic Church that was symbolically false in its repressive maleness.

However, it was not quite as simple or uncontroversial a matter as Erasmus in his New Testament or Foxe in his 'Book of Martyrs' pretended. Even Luther knew that it was a risky thing to put the scriptures directly into everyone's hands. Erasmus, of course, wrote his wish list in Latin. So we must investigate the near-paradox that the Reformation, which released and energized the vernacular, was made possible by the movement we call Renaissance humanism, which was a Latin thing. Humanism was more than a desire to clean up the Latin language, to restore it to the excellence of its classical exemplars, although it was that. It carried the conviction that eloquence of expression, essentially the art of rhetoric, was more likely to convey those precious commodities, truth and virtue, than syllogistic logic, which was the basis of scholastic theology. Good men expressed themselves in good letters. Good letters made good men. But the good letters were, of course, Latin and Greek.

The reappropriation of Greek was one of the great achievements of the Renaissance. Erasmus's New Testament of 1516 was published in Greek, a first, with a new translation into

Latin, Erasmus's own, on the facing page. There was consternation among traditional, conservative churchmen. Quite apart from scripture supplanting the authority of the Church, it was no longer the received scripture of a thousand years, Jerome's Latin translation, which we know as the Vulgate. Yet what Erasmus called the *Novum Instrumentum* was dedicated to Pope Leo X, and in later editions he was able to print a letter of papal commendation: 'We take much pleasure in your endeavours . . . and hope it will help theology and the orthodox faith. God will reward you.'

Hebrew, too, was discovered. To acquire this key to the front door of the Old Testament, Christian scholars were dependent on learned Jews. In 1506 Johannes Reuchlin published his ground-breaking *De rudimentis Hebraicis*, only to find himself in a fire-fight with a poisonous brew of theological conservatism and anti-Semitism. For some years the Reuchlin business was much bigger than the Luther affair; indeed, the fuss about Luther was at first seen as merely one of its offshoots. Reuchlin's enemies were mocked in one of the greatest spoofs of all time, the *Letters of Obscure Men* (*Epistolae Obscurorum Virorum*), seventy epistles purporting to be written by the ridiculous Dominicans of Cologne. Erasmus laughed so much he almost did himself an injury. Luther was not amused.

It is time to become better acquainted with the high priest of this revolution in language and communication, Erasmus of Rotterdam, which is where he was born, but better described by one of his biographers as Erasmus of Christendom, who in the persona he claimed for himself was a new Jerome. Erasmus was born in either 1466 or 1469, outside of wedlock, which has given psychohistorians a field day and a novelist a plot, the Victorian author Charles Reade's *The Cloister and the Hearth*. Erasmus was his Christian name, 'Roterodamus' the best he could manage as a patronym. He also added 'Desiderius', the name of one of Jerome's correspondents. He died in 1536, by which time his world had changed.

Erasmus was neither the first nor the most learned of Renaissance humanists. He followed in the footsteps of the pioneering Lorenzo Valla, (c.1406–57) and applied to the Bible and the great Greek and Latin Fathers of the Church Valla's philological techniques, which had exposed as a medieval forgery the Donation of Constantine, the title deeds of the temporal sovereignty of the pope. He was also indebted to Rudolf Agricola (1444–85), a fellow Netherlander and a kind of intellectual grandfather, since Agricola taught the teacher who taught Erasmus. Agricola has been called 'the father of Humanism' by an authority for whom Erasmus was 'the prince of the humanists'. Erasmus's productivity was stupendous, the massive editions of the Fathers alone serving to make the point that he was much more than the equivalent of a journalist writing for the reviews and the Sunday papers, although in the twenty-first century that was one of the things that he would have been. His erudition was immense, but by modern standards uncritical, and the text of his Greek New Testament was inferior to that of the multilingual Bible known as the Complutensian Polyglot, prepared under Spanish auspices (1514–17, but only published in 1522), 'Complutum' being the university city of Alcalá.

However, Erasmus was by far the most famous scholar of his day, the result in part of a considerable gift for self-advertisement. We hear of a man in Switzerland who boasted that he had been pointed out in public as someone who had received a letter from Erasmus, whose correspondence (twelve volumes in the superb edition by P. S. Allen) was indeed public property. One of his *Colloquies*, little playlets that served as Latin without

tears for schoolboys all over Europe (a hundred editions in
Erasmus's own lifetime), was set in a brothel and Erasmus, who
seems to have been all but sexless and descended from a long
line of maiden aunts, enjoyed the joke when one of the girls
says, 'Oh yes, Erasmus is well known here.'

Erasmus made his name with his *Adagiorum Collectanea* or
Adages (1500), a collection of 818 proverbs, which went through
twenty-seven editions in his lifetime, and which was indicative
of a knowledge of classical literature in something like its
entirety. In 1508 it became *Adagiorum Chiliades*, now comprising 3260 proverbs with the Greek ones printed in Greek.
Eventually the total was 4251, a wide window on the mentalities of the ancient world. Soon the work was extended to
include essays on such aphorisms as 'War is sweet to those who
do not know it' ('Dulce bellum inexpertis') and 'Kings and fools
are born, not made' ('Aut fatuum aut regem nasci oportere').
Later reduced to shorter epitomes, the *Adages* was a standard
reference book for Rabelais in France, Cervantes in Spain, and
Shakespeare in England. People still employ quotations from
Shakespeare without knowing that they were borrowed from
Erasmus, who took them from the classics, which in many
cases were merely enshrining popular, proverbial wisdom. 'A
necessary evil', 'to squeeze water out of a stone', 'there's many a
slip betwixt cup and lip', 'let the cobbler stick to his last': all
these and many more familiar old saws are to be found in
Erasmus.

Another best-seller was *The Praise of Folly* (*Encomium
Morae*, which involves a pun on the name of Thomas More).
This was a rhetorical hall of mirrors in which every rule was
inverted in order to laugh at human frailty and yet still be
serious. What is more foolish than sex, and yet only love makes
the world go round. Folly is a woman, occupying the pulpit

(unheard of), praising herself (not allowed). So when Folly makes fun at the expense of Christ, who made himself a fool for our sakes, what are we to make of that? It is an example of what is called the 'Cretan paradox': 'A Cretan said, "All Cretans are liars."'

Erasmus was an entertaining writer, at work on the eve of events that would drive laughter out of the world. But at the same time he was in deadly earnest. Luther's prince, the elector Frederick, said that he was a wonderful little man: 'You never know where you are with him.' Luther himself said that Erasmus was an eel whom only Christ could catch. But there was nothing slippery about *Enchiridion militis christiani*, the handbook (or dagger) of the Christian soldier, which encapsulated what Erasmus liked to call 'the philosophy of Christ'. This improving and utterly sincere text, which harks back to the *Imitatio Christi*, was to become popular throughout Europe.

The most often repeated cliché about Erasmus is that he laid the egg that Luther hatched. Twenty years after his death, all his works would be placed on the Index of Prohibited Books by that fierce pope of the incipient Counter-Reformation, Paul IV, although not everyone took much notice. Historians and theologians have never stopped arguing over the question of whether Erasmus was a friend or an enemy of the Church that disowned him and whether – forget about Luther – he could have been the leader of a different kind of Reformation. Erasmus was a merciless and often satirical critic not only of ecclesiastical abuses but of the more gullible and superstitious of contemporary religious practices. Among the *Colloquies*, 'A Pilgrimage for Religion's Sake' takes us to England's most important shrines, Walsingham and Canterbury. At Walsingham, Erasmus was shown the Holy House, a replica of Jesus's home in Nazareth, which was believed to have been transported to Loreto in Italy by returning crusaders and was thought to be possibly a miraculous structure in its own right. 'Inspecting everything carefully, I inquired how many years it was since the little house had been brought there. "Some ages," he replied. "In any event," I said, "the walls don't look very old." He didn't dissent. "Even these wooden posts don't look old." He didn't deny they had been placed there recently, and the fact was self-evident.' The greatest historian of the English monasteries and their dissolution believed that Erasmus was a corrosive influence that helped to bring about their downfall.

St Thomas More, too, had some fun at the expense of religious rackets, and no one has ever accused More of betraying the Church. However, this kind of thing would read differently once Martin Luther had blown his whistle. Erasmus was thought by some to be on Luther's side, and there were attacks from the pulpit to that effect, while others urged him to make it clear that this was not the case by writing a book against Luther. It was inevitable that these two titans should clash, although the literary battle was delayed until 1524-5. Coleridge would write: 'Such utter unlikes cannot but end in dislikes and so it proved between Erasmus and Luther.' In the end Erasmus had to stay with the Church. But there was no insincerity in his denunciation of Luther's doctrine, either in its manner or its matter. He saw in Luther a new version of the theological rancour and violence for which he had attacked the scholastics and mendicants, and which he believed led away from rather than towards a simple Christian profession.

It is impossible to imagine Erasmus without the printing-press. Indeed, a kind of materialist reductionism might regard him as no more than a product of the invention by Johann Gutenberg of book production by means of movable type. That was in the 1450s, and it has been estimated that by 1500 some twenty-seven thousand titles, three-quarters of them in Latin, had appeared from presses across Europe. The medium was the message in the sense that the printers were eager for saleable copy, and Erasmus, and Luther too, learned to write to demand. One authority on these matters has proposed that it was not the Renaissance but printing that changed the world. We hardly know what the Renaissance was, except as a somewhat diaphanous idea, whereas we can handle and weigh the products of the printing-press, which had a huge impact on both learned and unlearned. The learned could now pursue their scholarly and polemical agendas in ever larger libraries, reducing the need for travel, and with the aid of indexes, bibliographies and variant editions, they could compare, collate and edit. It was the greatest change for the world of learning since the paginated codex replaced the scroll. And print put many more of the unlearned, whether themselves literate or not, under the spell of print rather than of purely oral tradition. Soon something as apparently oral and traditional as the legend of Robin Hood would be fed back into the orality of folktales from printed ballad texts. The Bible, too, would become familiar terrain, far better known than it is to most of us today.

Come the sixteenth century, print and the native languages of Europe were in a state of advancing symbiosis. If language made for shared identities, including national identities, print constructed a common vernacular language that was imposed on an infinite number of very local dialects (which are still with us). Those who virtually invented the literary languages of the future, Luther for Germany, Tyndale for England, John Calvin for France, were expert linguists who brought their Latin, Greek and even Hebrew to bear on the task. Tyndale was at first optimistic as a translator of Hebrew – 'In a thousand places thou needest not but to translate it into English, word for word'

– although as the going got tougher he found that his confidence in the perfect affinity of Hebrew and English was somewhat misplaced. Luther, too, wrote, 'Dear God, it is such hard work and so difficult to make the Hebrew writers speak German!' – but he succeeded, although while the New Testament was translated in eleven weeks the Old Testament took him and his assistants twelve years.

The German knight and humanist Ulrich von Hutten (1488–1523) came to a moment in his life when he resolved to write no more in Latin but only in his own language, a gesture of Renaissance patriotism. On the other hand, the no less patriotic Conrad Celtis (1459–1508) uttered only in Latin, in which he claimed that Germans were more eloquent, more civilized, than the Romans. Others, Luther included, whose own defiantly German speech had rubbed off on Hutten, were happy to write in German or Latin as circumstances demanded. The membrane between the ancient and modern languages was permeable. Thirty thousand new words, mostly of Latin origin, entered the English language between 1570 and 1630, more than at any other time in history. English survived this massive linguistic immigration and remained English, but it was now an English able to cope with the intricacies of politics and science – and religion.

Everywhere, the vernacular Bible was the most important vehicle for what we may call cultural nationalism, especially, of course, for Protestants. That the Bible was translated into Welsh (1588) was perhaps the main reason why the language and literature of Wales have survived only a stone's throw away from such English-speaking cities as Bristol and Liverpool. The fact that in Scotland the Bible was never printed in that version of English known as Lallans reduced the standing of Scots as a literary language. England itself was a special case. Whereas there had been eighteen editions of the Bible in German before Luther (fourteen in High German, four in Low German), a Dutch Bible when Erasmus was still young, and a Czech Bible in 1488, no part of the Bible had been printed in English before Tyndale published his complete New Testament in 1526, and that was when he was an exile, using a foreign press, at Worms. The first complete English Bible had to wait until 1535, a year before Tyndale, whose work it mostly was, was strangled and burned as a heretic near Brussels. The reason for this artificial situation was the presence in England of the endemic Wycliffite heresy, which sustained itself with a late fourteenth-century translation by a disciple of Wyclif, portions of which circulated from hand to hand among those who read it in secret conventicles.

Hence the strident insistence of Tyndale on the right of the English people to have the Bible in their own language. God had spoken to the Children of Israel in their own tongue through the law and the prophets. The apostles, too, had preached in the mother tongue. 'Why may not we also?' When attempts were made to lure him back into Henry VIII's England, Tyndale told a government agent that if the king would only grant his people what many other peoples already had, their own Bible, he would never publish another word. He would, as it were, cease to exist. And although Tyndale never did return, that is more or less what happened. He was soon all but forgotten, his work absorbed into the many English Bibles that the press produced in ever greater numbers over the next hundred years, many of them bearing the imprimatur of authority. The so-called Authorized Version of 1611 is ninety per cent Tyndale over those parts of the Bible that he had had time to translate before his tragic death, simply Tyndale in rather more stately dress.

The English, whose taste for scripturalism had already been

aroused in the fourteenth century in the age of Chaucer, when English first became a literary language, had been artificially starved of it. Now the English Bible became the prime text of the Reformation to an extent not seen anywhere else in Europe. A Victorian historian of the English people was able to say that by the lifetime of Shakespeare they had become the people of a book, the Book. Modern bibliographical research has borne out J. R. Green. Up to the mid-seventeenth century there were proportionally more Bibles printed and sold in England than anywhere else in Europe. The poetics of the seventeenth century, from John Donne to John Milton, is saturated with the richly tentacular tropes and metaphors of the Bible, while the speech of every day became peppered with scriptural phrases which rivalled Erasmus's proverbs: 'the burden and heat of the day', 'filthy lucre', 'God forbid', 'the salt of the earth', 'the powers that be', 'eat, drink and be merry' – all are Tyndale's inventions.

It was not, of course, only a matter of the Bible. The fact that from 1549 onwards (with a brief interruption under Queen Mary in the late 1550s) the worship of English parish churches was conducted entirely in English, according to the principle that it must be 'understanded of the people', helped to forge a strong bond between language and national as well as religious consciousness. By the mid-seventeenth century a large portion of the English nation was as strongly attached to the Prayer Book as to the Bible, which, strange as it may seem to moderns, was part of the reason why Charles I was able to raise a royalist army to fight against a Puritan-dominated Parliament.

However, if England was a special case it was not unique. Luther's German Bible was as large a landmark in the history of the German language as Tyndale was in English, the first work of art in German prose. Like Tyndale's, Luther's achievement was to pitch on a literary language that was close to colloquial speech, settling somewhere between the crudities of dialect and a language too elevated for ordinary mortals. He wrote: 'One must ask the mother at home, the children in the street, the man at the market, and listen to how they speak, and translate accordingly.' His Bible was a significant contribution to the triumph of the so-called High German of the south and centre over the Low German of the north and other dialects. A correspondent wrote with enthusiastic patriotism on the appearance of Luther's New Testament in 1522: 'It is to us Germans rather than to other nations that God has given his Divine Word.' This, too, became a book of the people.

But not only to us Germans! Almost all the emergent European nationalities acquired their own vernacular Bibles in the course of the sixteenth century, and in every case this marked the progress of standardized language at the expense of dialect. This was the significance of the great Bible printed at Kralice in Bohemia between 1579 and 1593, described as 'the finest example of the older Czech language'. Everywhere both the political authorities and responsible churchmen were nervous about letting the unlearned and semi-learned loose on a potentially dangerous book, especially when published with prefaces and notes that made the Bible a vehicle for one Protestant tendency or another. In England Henry VIII tried to avoid that danger by presenting the Bible as a manual of obedience to his royal self, and there was a similar situation in Sweden, where the New Testament was translated into Swedish in 1526 and the whole Bible in 1541. There was no consensual Bible in French to serve as the Bible of a French nation, but the emperor Charles V allowed the publication at Antwerp of bibles in both French and Flemish, provided they were purged of specifically Lutheran elements. There was even a Protestant Spanish Bible, a Castilian version that was the work of an ex-monk, Casiodore de Reina, but naturally it was printed not in Spain but in Basle (in 1569).

So the sixteenth century fully vindicates the claims of the late Adrian Hastings that 'texts can produce peoples' and that, among texts, the Bible is 'the prime lens through which the nation is imagined', 'a mirror for national self-imagining'.

4 *Luther discovers the Gospel and challenges the Church*

'That change I have here in this Story unfolded is such that no man who does clearly understand it can think of it without the utmost degree of Admiration and Wonder. Its beginning was small and almost contemptible; and one man alone, a while, bore the hatred and violence of the whole World.' So wrote, in 1555, the first official historian of the Reformation, Johann Sleidan, propagating the myth that these great events had the smallest beginnings in the protest of the obscure individual soon hailed as the German Hercules, Martin Luther. This was a replication of those biblical myths of human weakness transformed by divine strength, such as that of the shepherd boy David with his sling and five stones confronting Goliath. For Goliath, read the pope.

Luther claimed to have discovered, or rediscovered, something called the Gospel. What he found, and when he found it, and how original a departure this may have been, how the things going on in Luther's head and in his university lectures interacted with his public role as a critic of Church practice, together with the Church's negative response: these questions have sustained the Luther industry for many years. They are the reason why, at its most productive, over a thousand items have been published on Luther in a single year. Attention has centred on the *Turmerlebnis*, Luther's experience in the monastery tower. What and when was it? This small conundrum points to a larger question. What was the Gospel according to Luther? What is essential Protestantism?

Some of the answers are to be found in those who taught Luther his schoolroom theology, regardless of the fact that he later rebelled against them. It is hard to shake off altogether such early and formative influences. Luther's teachers were scholastic theologians of the tendency known as Nominalism, the pupils of Gabriel Biel (c.1420–95), founder of the University of Tübingen. Nominalists, a bit like modern deconstructionists, denied the existence of 'universals', or 'species', beyond the words we use to construct them. God could not be known to reason but only as a matter of faith. This was a threat to the whole edifice of scholastic theology erected by, for example, St Thomas Aquinas. So was that where Luther got his theology of blind, irrational faith? So some modern 'ecumenical' Catholics, who want to be friendly to Luther, have wanted to argue because it lets him off the hook and makes him the innocent victim of bad theology. But perhaps it was not bad theology at all. Nominalists taught that we know about God only what He chooses to tell us (revelation), which we must accept on trust. But we may trust that He is a consistent God who tells the truth and keeps His promises. To that extent Luther remained a Nominalist.

That, however, is not where Luther got his religion. The place to begin is not the university lecture room but, in a manner of speaking, at his mother's knee. Who was Luther's mother? Catholics briefed that she was a maid in a bathhouse (the same thing as a prostitute) who had casual sex with the Devil. But leaving that calumny aside, was she Margarethe (known as Hanna) Ziegler or Hanna Lindemann? Confirmation that she was a Lindemann, a family of most respectable burghers of the

Thuringian town of Eisenach, which produced lawyers, physicians and academics, professions pursued by Luther's first cousins, proves to be significant. Hanna Lindemann married beneath her when she became the wife of Hans Luther, a miner of peasant stock who had risen in the world, but only on borrowed money, to run a mine extracting copper from shale. In her father's house she would not have had to collect her own firewood. More important, though, was what her family was able to do for her son. Luther received an excellent education, at Mansfeld while he was still living at home, then briefly at Magdeburg (with the Brethren of the Common Life), and finally at Eisenach among his mother's relations, which sent this clever boy on his way to the University of Erfurt.

It was perhaps in church at Eisenach that Luther's religious sensibilities were first aroused. Sermons of the kind to which Luther would have been exposed were designed to harrow the heart. They were about sin and repentance. Salvation was by contrition alone. The greatest preachers of the age, like Geiler von Kaisersberg (1445–1510), for whom the magnificent pulpit was erected that still stands in the cathedral at Strassburg, knew that only God's free forgiveness was sufficient for salvation but believed that in such evil times it was best not to make too much of that. Better preach like John the Baptist, warn people to repent, flee from the wrath to come, bring forth fruits of repentance. Life is only a brief episode before death. As one preacher put it, 'The sinner is careening towards death.'

We may say that the Luther we know was formed by his father's ambition, which sent him to law school, and his mother's drastic piety, which after a close brush with death drove him away from the law and into the monastery ('St Anne help me! I will become a monk') Whether the evidence of the inner Luther will bear the Freudian interpretation put upon it by Erik Erikson's once famous *Young Man Luther* (the source of John Osborne's play *Luther*) is doubtful. But it would be absurd and a piece of inverted reductionism to suggest that Luther's quarrel was only with God and had nothing to do with his dealings with both his parents (Erikson did not know that Luther had a mother). Luther, above all theologians, knew that we live in our physicality and social relations, not in some segregated spirit zone.

The monastery was the beginning, not the end, of Luther's spiritual quest. He tells us of the extremes of asceticism to which he subjected himself in what he later believed to be a vain and counterproductive attempt to please a God who would never be placated. The sermons Luther heard and the theology he was taught made salvation a matter of God's grace, not something that could be bought with a virtuous life. But for grace to work it was necessary for a man to do what he could from his side of the equation: *facere quod in se est*. How could Luther know that he had ever tried hard enough? These anxious strivings became a solipsistic preoccupation, the soul, in Luther's vivid description, turned in upon itself, *curvatus in se*.

The German word Luther used of these struggles was more strenuous than any equivalent in English: *Anfechtungen*. 'Temptations' is not adequate. It is not easy for moderns to capture what it may have felt like to be exposed to the wrath of God. But if God assaulted his tortured conscience on one side, the Devil was at him on the other, and the Luther who struggled with Satan is even more inaccessible. It was a struggle that expressed itself in scornful, scatological ravings. 'But if that is not enough for you, Devil, I have also shit and pissed; wipe your mouth on that and take a hearty bite.' Yet the man who could deploy this sort of language, even in his sermons, was administering eleven monasteries of his order! We have all been told that Luther threw his inkpot at the Devil, but that he defecated on him has been concealed from us in most of the books. Sixteenth-century Germany, which called a turd a turd, has been sanitized.

Luther was helped out of this morass by his superior in the Augustinian order and, it would seem, spiritual director, Johann Staupitz, a distinguished academic and much sought-after preacher. It was Staupitz who taught Luther to see that true repentance does not end but begins with the love of God. The trick is not to make God love us, the wounds of Christ are sufficient evidence that he does, but for us to love God.

This was the beginning of what has been called a Copernican revolution. Whether, as seems likely, the source of this insight was St Augustine is a problem we can leave to the learned theologians. It is rather more certain that it was Staupitz who insisted that Luther take his doctorate and begin to teach theology in the brand new University of Wittenberg, where Staupitz was dean and professor of biblical theology. Luther had been teaching in the faculty of arts at Wittenberg since 1508, a stint interrupted by a journey to Rome that may, or may not, have shattered his worldview. Suffice it to say that he reacted as a good German Catholic might have been expected to react to the Las Vegas of its day, the Rome of the Renaissance popes. In 1512 Luther became a doctor of theology and succeeded the overworked Staupitz in his chair. Would it be fanciful to suppose that Staupitz saw that the cure to this young monk's spiritual malaise might lie in plenty of hard work? With very few absences, Luther would spend the next thirty years delivering his twice-weekly lectures on the Bible to generations of students. The Reformation happened between lectures.

Luther began with an attack on scholastic theology and its philosophical footings in Aristotle, which attracted about as much public interest as any other exercise in academic revisionism. Through a sustained exercise in the science of hermeneutics, he was now struggling with the meaning of the biblical text, for the students he taught and the people of Wittenberg to whom he preached on Sundays, but above all for himself. We know that his first lectures were on the Psalms, followed by Paul to the Romans, Paul to the Galatians, the Epistle to the Hebrews and so back again (in 1519) to the Psalms. Those who know anything about the Reformation will be aware that there is a point of punctuation along this road. It was in October 1517 that Luther wrote and posted his Ninety-Five Theses against the trade in papal indulgences. These were pieces of printed paper offering remission of the time to be spent in purgatory in expiation of their sins by both the living and those already dead, and they were being sold to settle the debts of a German archbishop and to fund the great rebuilding of St Peter's in Rome. As the jingle went, 'As soon as the coin in the coffer rings / The soul from purgatory springs': so people were assured by Johann Tetzel who was selling Pope Leo X's indulgences in Saxony, a brilliant salesman whose commission was twenty times a professorial salary plus expenses.

How did Luther's partly private struggle with the Bible relate to these more public events? When was the tower experience, if indeed we can pinpoint it as an event rather than a process? Was it before or after the indulgences affair? If before, then it was on that basis that Luther became a rebel against the prevailing religious system; if after, then his theology was driven by the publicity his protest had aroused and the need for further reflection on the issues it raised. In a version of the story favoured by some ecumenically motivated Catholics, Luther never did post the Ninety-Five Theses on the church door in Wittenberg and certainly not in a mood of defiance. He merely posted (in our sense of putting in the post) his legitimate concerns to his archbishop, the same Albrecht of Mainz in whose interest the indulgences were being sold. But, surprise, surprise, the archbishop took no notice. Luther was not heard, and the rest is history.

Luther referred to his breakthrough moment on several occasions. Usually this was in mealtime conversation, which suggests that the anecdote had taken the place of genuine memory, as the stories we tell about ourselves usually do. But always it had to do with a text in St Paul to the Romans, Chapter 1, Verse 17: 'For therein is the righteousness of God revealed from faith to faith: as it is written, The just shall live by faith.' Towards the end of his life, the story was told in greater detail. It was, Luther said, in 1519, when he had begun to lecture on the Psalms for a second time, that he at last got to the bottom of that text. Only then did he understand that God's righteousness was not an actively punitive righteousness but a righteousness with which God justifies us through faith. It was then that Luther felt that he had been reborn.

The problem for Luther scholarship is that Luther must have learned these things much earlier than 1519, perhaps when he first lectured on the Psalms (1513–15) or when in 1515 he started on Romans. There is no lack of evidence. Texts of these lecture courses have survived. But they pose more questions than they answer. Meanwhile critics have complained that Luther should have known all along what was no more than orthodox doctrine. But the fact is that Luther had to find a way out of the religion in which he had been brought up, which had moved so far in its emphasis on contrition as to suggest that salvation is actually earned.

It was one thing to discover that it is God who saves us, not we who save ourselves. But the essence of Luther's doctrine of justification went beyond this to the means by which we are saved. It could be that God's grace works on whatever slight capacity a man might have to turn towards Him, fanning the feeble spark into a flame, until in the end it is a man (Adam, as it were) progressively transformed in his nature by grace who stands before God. However, this, which in a nutshell is Augustine's doctrine and the essence of Catholicism at its most authentic, was not Luther's final and mature position. Augustinianism fused, in Luther's perception confused, justification and sanctification, which for Luther were two separate things. Luther would teach that we are saved by another righteousness, Christ's righteousness. Only faith, itself a gift from God, can take hold of this righteousness. Hence justification by faith alone, *sola fide*. This is something that happens all at once, *auf einmal*, not bit by bit, *stücklich*. It is like a marriage. Christ, the bridegroom, takes as His bride a wretched and depraved prostitute and at once she acquires His riches and He her wretchedness. The sinner does not cease to be a sinner, but is no longer seen to be a sinner. He is at one and the same time a sinner and justified: *simul justus ac peccator*.

It is not that good works are no longer necessary, but they are not necessary to achieve salvation, a selfish, slavish motive. Rather they are performed gladly, gratefully and naturally. The English Lutheran William Tyndale wrote that the question should not arise whether the justified man has to do good works, because he has done them already and is forever doing them, such is his nature. Luther's doctrine of justification by faith alone had freed mankind from morality, but equally it had freed man *for* morality. There is a timeless distillation of these insights in Luther's most appealing book, *The Freedom of a Christian* (1520): 'A Christian is a perfectly free lord of all, subject to none. A Christian is a perfectly dutiful servant of all, subject to all.'

No apology should be needed for descending, to that modest extent, into what will seem to moderns, even most modern Christians, redundant theological intricacies. For here was the essential difference between what would now take shape as Protestantism and Catholicism as it would be reconstituted by the Council of Trent: two versions of Western civilization. It was essentially an anthropological difference. What is a man? Was his creation in the image of God carried forward triumphantly in his salvation in Christ, which is what Counter-Reformation mannerist painting and exuberant baroque churches, expressive of what Luther called 'a theology of glory', tell us? Or was he a humble, receptive creature, nobody without the overwhelming grace of God, an idea that is reflected in the plainness and modesty of protestant places of worship, which are mere receptacles for the saving Word? It is the difference between Rubens and Rembrandt. Think of El Greco's *Burial of Count Orgaz* (in Santo Tomé, Toledo), where the pious nobleman dies surrounded by the Church Militant and is presented in heaven in his naked but perfectly formed humanity. Then think of one of Rembrandt's domestic interiors. The contrast is between a triumphant Church and a mundane, passive, receptive Church.

Yet it may be that this is not where Luther had arrived on 31 October 1517 when the Ninety-Five Theses were (or were not) 'posted'. Perhaps it was as a consequence of what happened to Luther after that initial protest that Western Christendom was to be split down the middle by a small but seminal point in theology. The Luther who had lectured on the Psalms and Romans may still have believed that the saving work of Christ is something that operates within ourselves, a matter of induced humility. To go down into the depths with Christ was a strong motif of late medieval Christianity, the suffering experienced inside, not 'extrinsic' and 'imputed'.

This was wholly consistent with Luther's attack on indulgences, which he characterized as a market in 'cheap grace'. Thesis after thesis reiterated the theme. 'Christians should be taught' ('*docendi sunt Christiani*'): 'Away, then, with those prophets who say to Christ's people, "Peace, peace!" when there is no peace' (Thesis 91); 'Good riddance to all of those prophets who say to Christ's people, "The cross, the cross!" when there is no cross' (Thesis 93); 'Christians should be exhorted to seek earnestly to follow Christ, their Head, through penalties, deaths, and hells' (Thesis 94).

This 'theology of the cross', as it has been called, remained a kind of ground bass to the music of Luther's theology, before as well as after whatever experience or insight may have superseded it. God is a *Deus absconditus*, a hidden God who wears a mask and is known only paradoxically, the baby in the manger, the man on the cross, the presence in the Eucharist. God is there in the tiresome routines of family life, in what the state does to criminals, in war. Luther would have found God in the Holocaust. He was not outside his world, although He had allowed it to fall under the Devil's sway, as a *Teufelsreich*, and He was visible within it only by faith. Whatever else we may want to say about him, and a recent biographer has called him 'a catastrophe in the history of Western civilization', Luther was a theological genius, the counterpoint to Johann Sebastian Bach in music.

What happened on 31 October 1517 has been compared to a man groping his way up a church tower in the dark, who hangs on to a rope only to find that he is ringing a bell that wakes up the whole town. Whether Luther only intended his Theses to initiate an academic debate, and whether or not he 'posted' them as a gesture of defiance, became irrelevant within a couple of months. They passed into the hands of the printers and were soon in the public domain all over Germany, in German as well as Latin. It was as if in the sixty years since its invention the printing-press had been treading water, waiting for this moment. Its output in Germany increased sixfold in the years between 1518 and 1524, and an astonishingly large proportion of what was produced consisted of things that Luther himself wrote: thirty titles, perhaps three hundred thousand copies. By March 1518 it was a little late for Luther to write to a friend: 'As for the Theses, I have certain doubts about them myself.'

Looking back from 1521 and the Diet of Worms, events moved forward with inexorable logic, a drama in a series of scenes. At first, a detached observer might have thought that this was nothing more than a spat between two gangs of monks, Luther's own order versus the Dominicans, who naturally sprang to the defence of their own, Friar Tetzel, the vendor of indulgences. But soon Rome was informed and Luther was called to account as a suspected heretic. He could have been sent to Rome in chains but instead was summoned to appear before a prince of the Church, Cardinal Cajetan, the general of the Dominicans, who was attending the imperial diet at Augsburg as papal legate, hoping to drum up support for a coalition to fight the Turks. Cajetan was the most distinguished theologian of his generation and was nonplussed as well as outraged when this German monk, instead of submitting, stood his ground and proposed to hold a debate. Luther was spirited out of Augsburg and back to Wittenberg in the nick of time.

That Luther survived to make his historic appearance at Worms had little to do with theology and everything to do with politics. The Holy Roman emperor (Kaiser Max) was dying and

Luther's prince, Frederick 'the Wise' of Saxony, was one of the imperial electors, someone whom Rome could not afford to offend if it wanted to avoid the election of another Habsburg. In June 1519, however, Maximilian's nephew, Charles V, was duly elected. Luther had been allowed to survive and destroy the Church by virtue of a moment in European politics that was soon over and forgotten. Frederick, perhaps persuaded by his secretary, Spalatin, a friend of Luther, was not prepared to throw to the wolves the most famous professor in his own university. Rome now sent a new emissary to deal with Luther, a shallow and emollient diplomat called Karl von Miltitz, one of those Germans who had been spoiled by Italy. Luther saw through Miltitz but agreed to tone down his public utterances.

The next and most critical of these set pieces was staged at Leipzig in July 1519: a full-scale disputation between an adroit debater, Doctor John Eck of Ingolstadt, and the Wittenbergers, an occasion presided over by the other Saxon prince, Duke George. Luther was not supposed to be on the bill for this performance, but when he took the floor, some days into the debate, the result was dramatic. Eck had shifted the agenda onto dangerous ground, the authority of the pope and whether it was divine or merely human in nature. Luther wanted to play the Greek card, appealing to the Churches of the East which were not obedient to the bishop of Rome. But one of Eck's more palpable hits was to bracket Luther with Jan Hus and it was now that Luther, far from dissociating himself from the Bohemian heretic, announced that among the articles of belief for which Hus and the Hussites had been condemned were 'many which are truly Christian and evangelical, and which the Church Universal cannot condemn'.

The gloves were now off. Eck drew up a formal indictment and sent it to Rome, and in June 1520 Pope Leo X issued a suspended sentence of excommunication in the papal bull *Exsurge Domine*. Even now Miltitz was hoping that things could be smoothed over. Before the papal bull arrived in Germany, Luther was persuaded to send the pope his *Freedom of a Christian* with an accompanying letter that went through some diplomatic motions. 'I freely vow that I have, to my knowledge, spoken only good and honourable words concerning you whenever I have thought of you.' But the mask soon slipped. 'I have truly despised your see, the Roman Curia, which . . . neither you nor anyone else can deny is more corrupt than any Babylon or Sodom ever was.' At about this time he wrote: 'Farewell, unhappy, hopeless, blasphemous Rome!'

The year 1520 saw the publication of two other manifestos that were tantamount to a declaration of war. *An Open Letter to the Christian Nobility of the German Nation concerning the reform of the Christian Estate* (which sold out the initial print-run of four thousand copies in five days and rapidly went into sixteen further editions) called upon the temporal rulers of Germany, from the emperor downwards, to undertake a comprehensive reform of abuses beginning with what Luther called 'the Romanists'. This was in the time-honoured tradition of grievance literature, but the theological basis of the appeal was new and revolutionary. The distinction between popes, bishops, priests, monks and nuns as 'religious', and princes, lords, artisans and peasants as 'secular', was spurious. 'For all Christians whatsoever really and truly belong to the religious class, and there is no difference among them except insofar as they do different work.' From this affirmation would come such characteristic features of Protestantism as ministry rather than priesthood, and a married ministry at that, and the responsibility for religious affairs that would be assumed by protestant governments.

More openly destructive of the entire fabric of Catholicism was the book called *The Babylonian Captivity of the Church*, which denounced the Church's seven sacraments as a system of 'miserable servitude'. The argument was a series of logical deductions from the sovereign principle of justification by faith. The Mass in particular, the pulsating heart of medieval catholic belief and practice, was not a work but an object of faith and it was a total misconception to call it a sacrifice offered to God. Penance, too, was a form of tyranny, the penitential system 'a factory of money and power'. It was against this drastic manifesto that Henry VIII wrote his *Assertion of the Seven Sacraments*, which earned him and all his successors to the present day the papal title Defender of the Faith, proving that history is not without a sense of humour.

As these books were going to the printers, the papal bull was published in Germany and bonfires were being made of Luther's writings. On 10 December at nine o'clock in the morning there was a counter-demonstration in Wittenberg. A fire was lit and onto it were thrown volumes of the canon law, sundry papal decretals, and books by Eck and other enemies of Luther. Last of all, Luther himself came forward and threw onto the flames the bull of excommunication. Three weeks later Pope Leo X issued a further bull by which Luther was definitively excommunicated.

Within four months Luther stood before Charles V at Worms, where so many of his books were piled up in a window recess that the emperor was reluctant to believe that one man could have written them all. According to a deal worked out in advance between Charles and the papal nuncio, Aleander, Luther was to be denied the opportunity to debate or even to defend himself. He would merely be told to recant his heresies. Surprisingly, he now asked for and obtained a day's remission to consider the matter. The next day, 18 April, at six o'clock in the evening, in a crowded and stiflingly hot room in which only the emperor was allowed to sit, Luther made a dignified but uncompromising speech in both Latin and German, which drew from the master of ceremonies the rebuke that he appeared to want to dispute things that he was obliged to believe without question. The Middle Ages had spoken. Now the Reformation retorted, not with the famous 'Here I stand', which is probably apocryphal, but with these no less memorable words: 'Unless I am proved wrong by the testimony of Scriptures or by evident reason I am bound in conscience and held fast to the Word of God . . . therefore I cannot and will not retract anything, for it is neither safe nor salutary to act against one's conscience. God help me. Amen.' Luther and all his aiders and abetters were now declared outlaws.

Whether the German princes, Luther's prince in particular, would execute the imperial edict was, given the nature of German politics, another question. The emperor honoured Luther's safe conduct, enabling him to return to Wittenberg, where, however, it was not intended that he should be safe. Before that there were some days of fruitless negotiation, which began the lifelong literary feud between Luther and his most energetic if not most intelligent antagonist, Johannes Cochlaeus, who would be mainly responsible for the demonization of Luther. ('Luther lusted after wine and women . . . He was a liar, a hypocrite, a coward and a quarreler', and, most surprising, 'he had not a drop of German blood in his veins.') Then, as he travelled home, Luther was taken hostage by friends and became a missing person, holed up in the castle of the Wartburg, looking down on Eisenach, a place where in his childhood he had picked strawberries. Here he suffered from depression and appalling constipation ('my arse has gone bad'), grew a beard, translated the New Testament and wrote so much else besides that one biographer has remarked, 'It was as though he built the pyramids in a year.'

Still to come was the *annus mirabilis* of 1525, which saw the great convulsion of the Peasants' War, Luther's marriage, and his battle of the books with Erasmus. But here we must leave Luther in order to investigate what was going on in other parts of the forest. When we return it will be with this question: we know (or hope that we know) what Luther was saying; but what was he heard to be saying, in Germany and beyond?

5   *Alternative patterns of reformation*

Without Martin Luther the sixteenth century might have seen a series of convulsive movements of religious reform, more than one schism in what had been the seamless coat of the Catholic Church, and to these the blanket term Reformation might have become attached. It would not have been the same Reformation. But at the same time the Reformation was not simply Lutheran. Luther was not an antipope. This is what he said to the Strassburgers at a theological summit in 1529: 'I am neither your lord nor your judge. What you teach in Strassburg is no concern of mine. As long as you persist in not accepting my teaching, I cannot tolerate you as my disciples.' (With Luther self-assertion and self-abnegation were two sides of the same coin.) But he had limited control over events and opinions. It was not so much Luther as his colleague Philipp Melanchthon, professor of Greek at Wittenberg and *praeceptor Germaniae*, who introduced the principle of dogmatic order and uniformity in the Augsburg Confession (1530), the beginning of a lengthy and messy process that refined and defined Lutheranism, culminating in another of history's jokes, the *Book of Concord* (1580). Not for nothing did Shakespeare refer to 'spleeny Lutherans'.

At first every German city, and the Reformation was something that happened mostly in the towns, was a law unto itself, every preacher and pamphleteer a reformer according to his own lights. Other regions with other cultures invented other patterns of reformation, especially Switzerland, which drew into its orbit south-west Germany including the Strassburgers. The so-called Anabaptists hived off in a variety of directions, cutting loose from the constraints of law and government, so that the modern catch-all label 'radical' may fit them best. And soon there was a new theological planet that exerted a force of gravity greater even than Luther's: the Frenchman John Calvin, whose powerful mind took over Geneva. In the play, Hamlet was interrupting his studies at Wittenberg, which makes sense since Denmark (and all of Scandinavia) had turned Lutheran. By Shakespeare's time, however, Calvin's Geneva was a more powerful magnet, the centre of the Comintern of its day. Between the Calvinists, or Reformed, and the Lutherans, or Evangelicals, a great gulf became fixed that not even the common predicament of protestant Christians in Nazi Germany would be able to bridge.

An early deviant was one of Luther's colleagues, and in some respects his senior, in the university and church of Wittenberg, Andreas Bodenstein von Karlstadt (1486–1541). Karlstadt was a loose cannon, a man full of ideas which were always changing, but he was no Luther and that rankled. It was Karlstadt who challenged Johann Eck with the overkill of no less than 405 theses, provoking the great debate at Leipzig, where he was upstaged by Luther. In Wittenberg in 1521–2, during Luther's absence in the Wartburg, Karlstadt (and Melanchthon, it was not all Karlstadt's fault) went into action: a radical simplification of the Mass celebrated in everyday dress, iconoclasm, a programme of municipal reform and, for himself, marriage to a girl of fifteen. The Wittenberg Movement was precipitate and illegal, but Karlstadt was only anticipating what would become the programme of reformation in many cities. What was untypical was Luther's reluctance to turn his ideas into radical action; not until 1526 would he publish an order of the Mass in German. Then Luther returned, Karlstadt was repudiated and humiliated, and he retired to the country, where he put on peasant costume, stood rounds in the pub and asked to be called 'Neighbour Andreas'.

There followed a process of progressive radicalization, which Luther put down to naked ambition. Karlstadt launched a series of attacks on the doctrine and practice of the Mass, denying what was still precious for Luther, the real presence of Christ's body and blood in the bread and wine. Again, most Protestants outside the Lutheran lands of Germany and Scandinavia would come to share that view. No more than Luther is Karlstadt imaginable without the printing-press, which eagerly consumed his copy: ninety books, 213 editions. When Karlstadt found himself in the middle of the Peasants' War and compromised, Luther rescued him and took him into his own house. But Karlstadt could never be pinned down and he later set off on another peripatetic career, always accompanied by his long-suffering but ultimately broken wife: Frisia, Basle, Zürich and back to Basle, where he died of the plague in 1541, a member of the awkward squad to the last. Yet it was Karlstadt rather than Luther who pointed to much of the future character of Protestantism.

If Karlstadt was an almost comic figure, Thomas Müntzer (c.1489–1525) was altogether tragic. He, too, began as some kind of 'Martinian' (the early label for a Lutheran) and was in Wittenberg that fateful autumn of 1517, although he drew his intoxicating religious ideas from many other sources including the late medieval mysticism that nourished Luther's piety and underlay his 'theology of the cross'. In the restless crucible of Müntzer's intellect and soul these elements (which even included the Koran) fused in a religion of drastic catharsis, a standard against which he judged Luther as 'Brother Soft-Life', peddler of an easy faith without works or suffering. This was unfair. Müntzer knew nothing of Luther's own spiritual torments and his Luther was a caricature, sniffing a bunch of carnations in that hot smelly room at Leipzig.

Just what it was that turned Müntzer into an angry young man we shall never know, but in 1521, while Luther was otherwise engaged at Worms, we find him at the forefront of upheavals in the industrial town of Zwickau that made the Wittenberg Movement look like a vicarage tea party. Müntzer fell in with a group of autodidact 'prophets' led by a clothier called Nikolaus Storch, and whether he influenced the prophets or they him gives his biographers something to argue about. The leading Zwickau preacher, with whom Müntzer had quarrelled, called him 'a man born for heresies and schisms'. He took himself off to Prague, where he issued a manifesto that attacked those scribes and pharisees whose religion was all in the letter, and had much to say about what he called the Elect Friends of the Word of God. 'God will do marvellous things with his Elect, especially in this land', Bohemia, the wellspring of Hussite bolshevism. The manifesto proved a damp squib and Müntzer went back to Saxony, where his charisma took over the rather lawless little town of Allstedt.

What Müntzer built at Allstedt was important and pioneering: a church service in German complete with hymns, a thing of real merit, and a covenanted league of his closest followers, 'real' Christians. This was as controversial as it was sensational, and brought Müntzer under scrutiny at the highest level. So it was that he preached the most remarkable of all sermons in a century resounding with sermons, his famous *Fürstenpredigt*, to an audience consisting of the princes of Electoral Saxony, who had fallen over backwards to give him a fair hearing. The princes could not have enjoyed being compared to eels, who 'immorally in one great heap' had coupled with snakes, 'the priests and all the evil clerics'. They were told that God had put the sword of righteousness into their hands (Romans 13) but that if they failed it would be taken away from them.

Soon Müntzer was on the run again, climbing over the town walls under cover of darkness, leaving behind his wife, his child, his papers, embarking on more journeys. At Mühlhausen, a free imperial city noted for its beer, he preached in the middle of a rebellion that sacked the monasteries of the town and drove out the mayor and city council. He founded another covenanted band, the Eternal League of God, with a banner carrying a painted rainbow and the slogan 'The Word of the Lord Abideth for Ever'. These local disturbances merged with something much larger, the Peasants' War, in which Müntzer became an incendiary if peripheral force. His version of the Gospel had long been chiliastic and violent, at least in its language, with much talk of harvests, sickles and threshing-floors. Now, as he parted further and further from reality, it took on the more distinctly social overtones that enabled the German Democratic Republic to hail Müntzer (anachronistically) as the leader not only of a proletarian reformation but of a social revolution. His letters resound with the clamour of battle: 'Rataplan! rataplan! rataplan! time's up! ... Smite, cling, clang, on the anvil of Nimrod!' The insurgents, including elements of the elect bands from Allstedt and Mühlhausen, gathered at a place called Frankenhausen. It proved to be no stronghold but a death trap, called 'Blood Alley' for centuries to come. Müntzer assured his little Gideon's army of three hundred that they were invincible – and then himself took refuge in an attic where, after the slaughter of perhaps six thousand out of eight thousand peasants, he was discovered, tortured and, back at Mühlhausen, beheaded. The late Gordon Rupp, who succeeded in getting under Müntzer's skin, believed that, while he was not Marx or Lenin born before time, with Müntzer 'we come nearer than in any other reformer to contact with the smothered undercurrent of medieval pain and injustice'.

Meanwhile, an altogether different radical alternative to Luther's Reformation was taking shape in Switzerland, that unique coalition of confederate peasant republics and cities that was the exception to prove every rule about sixteenth-century Europe, and which as its main industry supplied the great powers of the age with their mercenary armies. Huldrych Zwingli (1484–1531), a native of the Alpine valley of Toggenburg in the canton of St Gall, was chaplain to one such battalion and saw action at the dreadful battle of Marignano (1515) where ten thousand Swiss were killed by French artillery. That made him the kind of patriot who opposed the mercenary tradition. This, and a programme of study that involved exposure to the humanism of 'good letters' in Basle, Bern, Vienna and Basle again, made Zwingli the kind of reformer he was, not at first 'religious' in the intense sense we associate with Luther: no 'tower experience' in his case.

Erasmus really did lay the egg that Zwingli hatched. In his first job as a parish priest, at Glarus (in 1506), Zwingli sat up all night mastering the New Testament in Greek. 'Reformation' for Zwingli came to mean total conformity to the Word of God in scripture. At the popular pilgrimage centre of Einsiedeln (in 1516) he became known as an elegant preacher in the new style, which led two years later to his appointment as people's priest in the Grossmünster in Zürich, the nearest thing that Switzerland had to a capital and the scene of occasional talking shops (not quite a parliament). Here he mounted the pulpit on 1

January 1519, his thirty-fifth birthday, and announced that he would break with tradition in preaching the New Testament from end to end, chapter by chapter. The Old Testament came next, as Zwingli added Hebrew to his toolkit. At the heart of the new church order in Zürich would be 'prophesying', a daily exercise in scriptural exposition from the original tongues, on which budding preachers cut their teeth, a practice imitated in Elizabethan England.

The Bible was now in charge of whatever was to happen in Zürich. The position of people's priest in cathedrals and the great collegiate churches, ruled by their wealthy clerical chapters, had been a relatively lowly one. The Word of God changed all that, making it a role of prophetic and quasi-episcopal authority. But Zwingli almost failed to make his thirty-sixth birthday. He found himself at death's door. Recovery from the brink brought the religious experience his life had hitherto lacked. 'I am your vessel, to use or to discard,' God was told in Zwingli's 'Plague Song'.

Now came a programme of change in religious practice more drastic than anything that Luther had contemplated. It began, modestly enough, with the deliberate eating of some sausages in Lent, but this was symbolic of the liberty of Christians to follow the dictates of scripture – alone. Merely human traditions were to be discarded. Soon Zwingli married, and he informed his bishop that this was indeed marriage, his wife was not the concubine or 'housekeeper' that most Swiss clergy kept at the back of the house. And now everything 'Roman' was called in question: indulgences, penitential works, pilgrimage, the worship of saints, the monastic life.

This was not a programme imported from Wittenberg, and there was less hesitation, no nonsense, as we might say, about Zwingli's agenda. On the other hand, in contrast to the exploits of Karlstadt and Müntzer, everything was done with due respect for the government of a well-run city. Progress was made in disputations held (in German) under magisterial authority. The result, by April 1525, was the end of the Roman Mass. The Easter Communion was administered not from an altar but from a simple wooden table, in wooden vessels. The words were those of the institution of the Last Supper in the Bible, and the people received wine as well as bread, taken to them where they sat. There were now only two sacraments in Zürich: baptism and Communion. The ministry of pastors replaced holy orders and episcopacy. Marriage became a civil ceremony. The differences between this, the beginnings of the Reformed tradition, and Lutheranism, even in the layout and aesthetics of church interiors, will be obvious to anyone who undertakes a church crawl from north Germany to protestant Switzerland, although the original Zwinglian style was more austere than anything to be seen today: whitewashed walls, clear windows, the plainest furnishings, no organs.

The essence of Zwinglianism, indeed what would serve to define it, was Zwingli's belief in what happens, and does not happen, in what Christians have variously called the Eucharist, the Mass, Holy Communion, the Lord's Supper. For Zwingli this was simply a commemoration of Christ's giving of himself; it was all in the mind, but mind and spirit were assisted by something physical, the eating and drinking of those same 'elements' that Jesus had distributed at the Last Supper. Yet they remained bread and wine. To assert that they 'became' the body and blood of Christ was both unnecessary and absurd. Christ in his humanity had ascended into heaven where he was seated on the right hand of God the Father. He could not also be in the bread and wine, and to suppose otherwise was to misunderstand the nature of a God who was to be worshipped 'in spirit and in truth'. As for Christ's words to his disciples, 'This is my body,' they were no more to be understood literally than other statements such as 'I am the true vine.' They were an interpretation, not an equation. The idea had spread to Switzerland from some of the New Devotionists in the Netherlands that by 'is' should be understood 'signifies'. Someone has made a lengthy list of the many meanings read into those simple words *'Hoc est corpus meum.'* Johannes Huszgen ('house lamp'), who called himself Oecolampadius (1482–1531), a learned Erasmian Protestant and the reformer of Basle, whose views on this question were influential, leant towards Zwingli's opinion but preferred 'is a signification of' to 'signifies' as it drew attention to the materiality of the elements and opened the way to an understanding that they could actually do something for the recipient. This was a pointer to where Zwinglianism would finish up.

For Luther such opinions were anathema. They went against his reading of scripture, his Christology, his understanding of 'flesh' and 'spirit', above all his craving for objective certainty. Christ's presence could not be made to depend upon having nice thoughts about him. As early as 1520 and *The Babylonian Captivity of the Church*, Luther had rejected transubstantiation (the catholic doctrine of a change effected by priestly consecration in the 'substance' of the eucharistic elements while the 'accidents' of appearance remain the same), but he continued to believe in the real presence, not because of some philosophical notion called 'consubstantiation' (a word he never used) but because Christ said it and therefore one must believe it. The flesh and the blood on the altar: that is almost the only place where God meets with us, where we receive into our mouths, chew and swallow, the baby in the manger, the man on the cross.

One of the most acrimonious of the Reformation pamphlet wars raged over these matters. Zwingli was stung to fury, and retaliation, by the fact that Luther had lumped him with Karlstadt in a diatribe called *Against the Heavenly Prophets* (1525), and indeed Luther continued to put it about that Zwingli and Oecolampadius were possessed by the Devil, worse than the papists. He called them *Schwarmgeister*, fanatics. But in 1529 politics brought all the leading players together around the same table, in the castle of the Landgrave Philip of Hesse above the city of Marburg. Earlier in the year the imperial diet, meeting at Speyer, had re-enacted the Edict of Worms and six evangelical princes and fourteen free cities had signed the protestation from which the word 'Protestant' derives. The Evangelicals were an exposed minority and Philip of Hesse, a man of action, was anxious to build up a defensive military league. All parties agreed that unity in faith must be a precondition for such an alliance. Zwingli also needed a military understanding. Switzerland was polarizing between the old faith and the new. Luther, however, came reluctantly to Marburg. Not only was his mind made up on the main point at issue but the idea of defending the Gospel with force went against the grain.

Famously, Luther began by chalking on the table, 'This is my body,' to which he added the comment, 'God is beyond all mathematics.' From that he never budged. At the end, when Zwingli with tears in his eyes asked for Luther's friendship he was met with, 'Call upon God, that you may receive understanding,' to which Oecolampadius retorted, 'Call upon him yourself, for you need it just as much as we!' The bare language deprives us of the banter, the body language.

The theologians agreed on fourteen other articles but not on this one. In the years that followed the difference hardened, with Lutheranism crystallizing around the dogma of the 'ubiquity' of Christ in His humanity which enabled Him to be present on every altar. When, in the 1550s, a group of English protestant exiles in Germany asked a leading Reformed theologian whether they could take their babies to be baptized in a Lutheran church they were told, no, baptism is a seal of faith and their faith is different from ours. Three hundred years later, some German Lutherans emigrated to South Australia rather than join a Union Church devised and imposed by Frederick William III of Prussia. They still make excellent wine in the Barossa Valley, where there is also a seminary faithful to its distinctively Lutheran heritage.

At the Diet of Augsburg in 1530, Lutherans and Zwinglians (including Strassburg) submitted different confessions of faith. The Protestants were in disarray even in their summit diplomacy. In Switzerland it soon came to war, if only a very small one, between the Protestants of the cities and the Catholics of the inner, forest cantons. Zwingli rode out from Zürich in armour and with a battleaxe. His body was found among the dead on the battlefield at Kappel. Someone looking down on it said, 'Well at least he was a good confederate.' Luther quoted Scripture: 'They that take the sword shall perish by the sword.' However, under the long and statesmanlike leadership of Zwingli's successor as chief pastor, Heinrich Bullinger (1504–75), Zürich continued to be a leader in Reformed Europe second only to Geneva, particularly in Elizabethan England – witness Bullinger's international correspondence, thousands of letters which modern scholarship is laboriously publishing.

The Zürich model of civic reformation was replicated in other Swiss and south German cities, usually under the prophetic ministry of an *antistes*, a new style of episcopacy. The old bishops had never been welcome in the cities and now they faded away like the Cheshire Cat. In Basle there was Oecolampadius, in Bern Berchtold Haller (1492–1536), a fat little man and no great leader but popular. Always things moved forward at a pace that the magistrates were willing to tolerate, but often under some popular pressure, the stages marked by disputations not designed to arrive at the truth but to implement what had already been decided. In Strassburg, one of the most important cities of the Empire, sitting on the Rhine at one of Europe's crossroads, was Martin Bucer (1491–1551) who is usually placed number four in the premier league of reformers, after Luther, Zwingli and Calvin.

Bucer was plucked out of a poor suburban parish to become people's priest in the cathedral, where he preached from Geiler's great pulpit sermons that, if they were anything like his books, were tediously prolix but passionate in their earnest moralism. He was part of an able team of reformers but *primus inter pares*. Bucer contributed to the Reformation a strong sense of the common good, which came partly out of his theology and partly out of humanism but was also a matter of civic values. His first book proclaimed in its title that a man should not live for himself but for others. The Church was above all a carefully ordered structure that enabled this to happen, and Bucer's idea of what a church should be was later communicated to Calvin, who was not prolix, and who put it into practice in Geneva. Bucer was also the first ecumenist of the Reformation, travelling hundreds of miles in search of consensus on the eucharistic question. By 1536 he and Melanchthon had achieved the Wittenberg Concord, reconciling the south German cities and Saxony. Even Luther did not absolutely reject it, although the Swiss cities did and worked their way towards the *Consensus Tigurinus* of 1549, essentially a Zürich–Geneva axis. Bucer's own position, close to Calvin's, was a version of Zwinglianism, and when, after the Schmalkaldic War, Strassburg had a Lutheran straitjacket imposed upon it he went into exile in England, where before he died he played a creative role in the English Reformation.

In contrast to the model of civic reformation there arose and spread a pattern of sectarian nonconformity which rejected the magistrate, and even the state itself, as having any place in true Christianity. These people were labelled, feared and persecuted as Anabaptists. The stigma was a little like the yellow star that Jews had to wear in Nazi Europe, since the law of the Christian Roman empire had imposed the death penalty on those who renounced their baptism as infants in order to repeat it, which is what 'Anabaptist' means. There was more to this movement than the question of the baptism of believers, but the rite did symbolize the kind of break with Christendom from which the so-called magisterial reformers held back. Anabaptists wanted to restore the Church to the status of a sect that it had held before Constantine.

If the modern world is ignorant of the Anabaptists it is not the fault of their historians, who are responsible for hundreds of books on the subject and even an encyclopedia. This is because various kinds of Anabaptists escaped decades, even centuries, of persecution by migrating to North America, where the Baptists became one of the largest protestant denominations, their number including Martin Luther King. Worldwide there were thirty-five million card-carrying Baptists in 1988.

Non-Baptist historians, especially Lutherans, cast Müntzer as the founding father of a chiliastic and always potentially violent movement. They are only partly wrong. Baptists, on the other hand, trace their pedigree from the pacific and apolitical Swiss Brethren, disciples of Zwingli who believed, with some cause, that by retaining infant baptism he had not gone far enough.

They, too, are partly right. The first executions of Anabaptists were in Zürich, the not inappropriate method being drowning in the River Limmat. By 1530 hundreds of Anabaptists had been executed in southern Germany, Austria and Switzerland, and in an age of martyrs and martyr books the annals of the Anabaptist martyrs far outweigh their Protestant and Catholic counterparts.

Anabaptism was never a Church. In 1527, however, there was a meeting at Schleitheim (near Schaffhausen) guided by leaders many of whom would soon be dead. The more militant tendency was covered by the last two of the seven Schleitheim Articles, which dealt with civil matters. True believers could not serve in the army or as magistrates and they could not swear oaths, which excluded them from active citizenship, particularly in Switzerland. But other leaders, notably Balthasar Hübmaier (1480/85–1528), the best early Anabaptist theologian, came to terms with 'the sword', although it was only in Moravia (now part of the Czech Republic) that Hübmaier was able, for a time, to achieve a tolerable modus vivendi with civil society. The split between the 'Schwertler' and 'Stäbler', sword-bearers and staff-carriers, persisted.

Nowhere in sixteenth-century Europe was it easy for sectarian separatists to remain in but not of mainstream society. Short of the neighbourly compromises that sometimes enabled peaceable Anabaptists to live a more or less normal life, especially in the Netherlands, there were two options. One we might call the 'Grapes of Wrath' option. The relatively empty lands of Eastern Europe beckoned, as California beckoned the desperate dirt-farmers of Oklahoma in the 1930s. The nobility of Moravia needed tenants and they were at first more open-minded than Steinbeck's Californian fruit-growers. Settlements

created by Jakob Hutter (1500?–36) experimented with commu-
nism, sharing goods and production. As with some modern
cults, these communes were not always a paradise on earth.
They were led by a succession of bishops, supported by elders or
'servants of the Word'. Hostile observers described leaders who
lived privileged lives, rode in coaches and drank the best wines.
Moreover, with Habsburg power never far away, these people
had no continuing city. Hutter was burned at the stake in
Innsbruck in 1536. Nevertheless, driven from pillar to post,
there are still Hutterites in the modern world, with settlements
as far apart as Paraguay and Shropshire.

The alternative was to take over and invert civil society in
apocalyptic anticipation of an expected Millennium. This is
what happened in the Westphalian city of Münster where the
local reformers had listened to the siren voice of Melchior
Hoffmann (1495?–1543), a travelling fur-trader and lay preacher
who was prophesying the imminent end of the world from a
prison cell in Strassburg. Hoffmann's Dutch disciples, including
Jan Matthijs (d. 1534) and Jan Bokelson, a butcher known as Jan
of Leiden (d. 1535), announced that Münster, not Strassburg,
was to be the New Jerusalem and proceeded to take the city
over. Hundreds of Anabaptists poured into Münster and all
citizens who refused baptism were threatened with execution
and expelled. Throughout 1534 and into 1535, as its bishop
besieged the city, none too competently, an extraordinary piece
of apocalyptic theatre was played out to its inevitably bloody
conclusion. Jan of Leiden sat on the throne of David with the
golden apple of global empire in his hand, ruling with operatic
pomp a polygamous realm in which there was competition to
see who could acquire the most wives. The king executed one
of his own sixteen (some said twenty-two) wives for being
cheeky and trampled on her body. At one point there was a

messianic feast in the cathedral square with food and drink served by the king and queen and psalm-singing. At last, with the assistance of Philip of Hesse, the city was taken. King Jan and other leaders were tortured with red-hot tongs, executed, and their bodies hung in cages suspended from the church tower, where their bones remained well into the age of Enlightenment. The cages are still there.

The frisson of Münster lasted for the rest of the sixteenth century. The English writer Thomas Nashe told the story in *The Unfortunate Traveller* (1593) to make a point about the dangers of sectarianism. 'Hear what it is to be Anabaptists, to be Puritans, to be villaines, you may be counted illuminate butchers for a while, but your end will be, Good people pray for us.' The Anabaptist cause was rescued from this debacle by a Dutch priest turned Anabaptist called Menno Simons (1496–1561), whose patient shepherding turned these shattered fragments of hoping and despairing humanity into a church, congregational, practising believers' baptism, eschewing public service but non-resistant. There are still upwards of a million Mennonites today.

6   *Calvin and Calvinism*

The myth of the Reformation as happening in an odd corner takes another form in the case of John Calvin (1509–64) and Geneva. The Geneva to which Calvin came in 1536 was a big place, of perhaps ten thousand inhabitants and larger than Zürich or Bern, but not one of the sixteenth century's great cities. There was one town up the hill where the notables lived and another down the bottom, like Lincoln in England. It had recently achieved its independence, an episode in some complex and very forgettable politics and military engagements involving its prince-bishop, the ducal house of Savoy, which thought that it owned the place, and the city of Bern, which after assisting a successful revolution in 1536 became its often unwelcome patron, controlling most of the hinterland of a city without a country. In the course of these events, Geneva had gone through the motions of becoming Protestant on the Bernese model but without having woken up to what that might entail. Geneva was an orphan, neither French nor fully Swiss, and something of an anomaly, the only city-state in Europe to establish and hang on to its independence in the sixteenth century, which indeed, it maintained until 1798. Its politics were turbulent, ridden with faction.

As for Calvin, he arrived in Geneva as a foreigner, unconnected with any of the families who ran the place. Someone referred to him as '*ille Gallus*' ('that Frenchman'), either forgetting or not caring about his name. But when the French cuckoo had finished with this nest it was very different. Many of the old bourgeois had been forced to leave, their houses now occupied by immigrants from France and other parts of Europe ostensibly motivated by religion. Soon the Scot John Knox, one of those asylum-seekers, would describe Geneva as the most perfect school of Christ that ever was in the earth since the days of the Apostles. Could any good come out of Geneva? Geneva, of all places, had become symbolic and mystical – Jerusalem or, a twentieth-century analogy, Moscow. Did the Reformation matter? For Geneva it did. It was Calvin's refugee Reformation that made it the city of Rousseau, of the League of Nations and, nowadays, of a whole host of sometimes useful international agencies.

Calvin's obscurity is compounded by the paucity of evidence relating to his life before Geneva (the reason being that he himself was a refugee), and here the contrast with Luther could not be greater. Calvin was naturally reticent so that there is no equivalent to Luther's garrulous table talk. So far as his recruitment to an evangelical faith was concerned, we have only two words, *subita conversio*, to set alongside all those *Turmerlebnis* stories. We know that such evidence is suspect, and indeed Calvin himself assures us that 'we are converted little by little to God, and by stages'.

Jean Cauvin ('Calvin' derives from the Latin form) was a native of Picardy, which for his detractors was sufficient explanation for his choleric personality. His grandfather was a bargee on the River Oise, his father a lawyer first serving and then falling out with the cathedral chapter at Noyon – an upward trajectory, a temperament. Calvin was intended for the priesthood and sent to study in Paris, first at the Collège de la Marche and then in the harsh environment of the Collège de Montaigu, which another alumnus, Rabelais, called 'a lousy college', but where Calvin honed an incisive theological intelligence. Perhaps his first alma mater mattered more, for it was there that he was taught by Mathurin Cordier, who perfected the language skills of the man destined to do for French what Luther was doing for German and Tyndale for English. One change in family fortunes transferred him to legal studies, which included exposure to the dazzling talents of the Italian Alciati, for whom the royal university of Bourges had been founded. Another turn enabled him to abandon the law and to return to Paris to immerse himself in humane letters, which included Greek and some Hebrew. In 1532, at the age of twenty three, came his first publication, a commentary on a work in which the Stoic philosopher Seneca had tried to moderate the behaviour of the Emperor Nero, *De Clementia*. It failed to make him famous.

What was it, more than a young scholar's ambition, that was soon to become the driving force for Calvin? In Paris he was surrounded by the leading figures of what historians of the French Reformation call the 'Prereform', a movement as safe as it was idealistic. But the world was changing and accusations of heresy were soon flying like paper aeroplanes. There were some burnings. Making bricks without much straw, we can make a plausible connection between some kind of religious conversion and this gathering crisis. When his friend Nicholas Cop, rector of the university and well connected, was forced to flee Paris in disguise after delivering a Lutheran sermon, Calvin decided that he, too, had better go on his travels. In October 1534, when the posting in Paris of handbills attacking the mass provoked repression on a wider scale, he decided that even France was too hot to hold him and he moved on first to Strassburg and then to Basle, where he published the first edition of the book with which he would change the world, his *Institutio Christianae Religionis*, Calvin's *Institutes*.

On one of these journeys Calvin by chance spent a night in Geneva. It was July 1536, two months after the city had taken an oath to live 'by the holy law of the gospel'. One of the preachers in Geneva was Guillaume Farel, an emotional man who was better at destroying the symbols of the old Church than building the new. His contribution to history was to know that Calvin possessed the talents that he himself lacked. Either he sought out Calvin or Calvin went to see him, but either way Farel threatened him with divine judgement if he were to go on his way and pursue the life of a private scholar. He must remain in Geneva. Or so the story goes. The choice between the active and contemplative life was a topos that all humanists had encountered in classroom exercises. Calvin: 'I felt as if God from heaven had laid his mighty hand upon me to arrest me.' For a second time this quintessential control-freak tells us that he himself was under control.

When Calvin was on his deathbed, in April 1564, he was at last prepared to reminisce: 'When I first arrived in this church there was almost nothing. They were preaching and that's all. They were good at seeking out idols and burning them, but there was no Reformation. Everything was in turmoil.' As soon as Calvin began to explain to the leading citizens what he meant by reformation he became central to the turmoil. In January 1537 he and Farel presented the magistrates with measures designed to secure 'a well-ordered and regulated church'. The sinews of this programme consisted of a crash course in instruction (catechizing), monthly communions, excommunication for recalcitrants, and an ecclesiastical tribunal to enforce discipline. Later a medical doctor in Heidelberg would give his name to the ideology to which Calvin proposed an alternative and which few Protestants before him had questioned: Erastianism, the doctrine that wherever there were Christian magistrates their jurisdiction and government was sufficient in ecclesiastical as well as civil affairs. 'Discipline', a coded word in the church politics of the later sixteenth century, meant not just discipline but the separate *magisterium* of ministers and officers of the Church. That was always going to be unpopular, and not only with secular magistrates like the syndics of Geneva. The city had not won its independence just to be told how to behave by a preacher. In March 1538 Calvin and Farel were told to leave the city – the precipitant, objections to Calvin's catechism.

The next three years were spent in Strassburg, where Calvin was married (to the widow of an Anabaptist with children), ministered to a small French congregation (more refugees), sent to the press a second edition of his Latin *Institutio* and prepared a French edition. The *Institution de la Religion Chrestienne* of 1541 marks the literary advent of the modern French language. Take the first sentence: 'Toute la somme de nostre saigesse, laquelle mérite d'estre appellée vraie et certaine saigesse, est . . . a scavoir la congnoissance de Dieu, et de nousmesmes.' If Calvin's prose had a classical sonority, it was also capable of a Tyndale-like vigour: living without government was to live 'pesle mesle, comme rats en paille', like rats in straw.

The Strassburg period brought Calvin into close contact with that city's commanding spiritual presence, Martin Bucer. Influence is admittedly a tricky substance for intellectual historians to handle, and enthusiastic admirers of Bucer have gone too far in attributing to the Alsatian reformer most of Calvin's creative ideas, as if he were merely Bucer's 'strong and brilliant executive'. But there can be no doubt that Bucer shared with Calvin his richly social doctrine of the Church and strengthened his conviction that 'discipline' was a necessity, one of its essential marks. For Bucer, no discipline, no community. Calvin put it differently. Where there is no discipline God is not honoured. That was the difference between them, for if Bucerism was about community, Calvinism was about God.

In 1541 Calvin was called back to Geneva. He wrote: 'There is no place under heaven that I am more afraid of' – and with good reason, since he now faced fifteen years in which he would have to slog it out in order to realize his vision of the city as a 'school of Christ'. Throughout those years Calvin was not a citizen, merely a council employee. There is no better example in history of the capacity of sheer moral conviction to prevail.

On the very day of his return Calvin asked the seigneurie that the church 'be set in order'. The outcome that he negotiated over the next couple of months was the religious constitution called the *Ordonnances ecclésiastiques*, a document of seminal importance and a model to be followed throughout Calvinist Europe. It defined the normative ministry of pastors, doctors, elders and deacons, and their functions; provided for weekly meetings of a company of pastors; called for what would become the Geneva Academy; and set up the consistory, a meeting of ministers and elders to oversee church attendance and morals.

Not that the magistrates capitulated to Calvin's prescriptive demands. Somewhere near the centre of his aspirations was frequent celebration of the Lord's Supper, if not weekly then monthly. But all he got was four a year. In this respect all Europe clung to old habits, in awe of the sacrament (superstition?) and deaf to the teaching that Christians should always meet with their Lord around his table. Calvin's deacons were stillborn; social welfare remained a civic matter. The Academy had to wait until 1559. The Ordinances did not empower the Church, in the shape of the consistory, to excommunicate, and the elder who was to preside over the consistory would always be a syndic with his baton, in the magistrates' perception not an elder at all but present by virtue of his civic office. Not until 1555 did the consistory secure the right to exclude from the sacrament, and not before 1560 did a syndic preside in his capacity as an elder. The authority of the consistory did not diminish that of the civil magistrate or ordinary justice. Calvin's legal skills would be called upon only in an advisory capacity, which was an influential role. He even drafted a civil constitution for the republic. But the notion that he was some kind of ayatollah who ran Geneva as a theocracy is a travesty.

What followed was a series of operatic storms in the Geneva teacup, almost as if the libretto was being written by a tabloid press. One storm concerned baptismal names. Calvin and his colleagues favoured biblical names and outlawed Claude, which was very popular in Geneva for both girls and boys but was associated with a nearby Catholic shrine. There were riots. A number of leading citizens and their families thought it patriotic to flout the Calvinist discipline. In their houses there was dancing, which was a punishable offence. History knows them as the 'libertines', although they called themselves 'children of Geneva' and denounced the French interlopers. Immigrants, of whom there were soon up to five thousand, were stealing jobs and pushing up rents. The leading libertines were members of the intermarried Favre and Perrin families. Calvin mocked Ami Perrin as 'our comic Caesar', but at the time Perrin was first syndic. They had to be smashed. When one of the libertines placed an anonymous note in Calvin's pulpit threatening him with assassination, he was identified, tortured and beheaded. But the snake was scotched, not killed, and it was only in 1555 that the Perrinists overplayed their hand by provoking a riot, which was interpreted as a coup. They were executed or exiled and their confiscated property used, symbolically, to fund the Academy.

There was also ideological opposition from some of the wild geese of the Reformation whom Geneva had attracted. Sebastian Castellio (1515–63), whom Calvin had made first rector of the Collège de Genève, revealed his propensity for dissidence by denying the canonicity of that erotic Old Testament poem, the Song of Songs. Later, after leaving Geneva, he came a public critic of its Church and a notable apologist for religious toleration, or at least for the opinion that killing heretics was wrong. Jérome Bolsec was a renegade catholic priest who challenged Calvin's doctrine of predestination. He was expelled and, having returned to Rome, wrote a defamatory biography of Calvin. Above all, there was Michael Servetus (c.1511–53), the greatest heresiarch of the time, a man of eclectic opinions including anti-Trinitarianism. His *Christianismi Restitutio* (1553) was a provocation by its very title and it was a gesture of mad defiance when he came to Geneva, perhaps encouraged by the political opposition to Calvin. He was already under a death sentence imposed in a French court. The council, anxious to appear orthodox, put Servetus on trial and called Calvin as first witness for the prosecution. After wide consultation with other Swiss cities, he was burned at the stake. This was by no means the only occasion when a protestant government executed a heretic. Queen Elizabeth of England burned some Dutch Anabaptists, and in 1612 James I sent to the stake two men whose views resembled those of Servetus. Nevertheless, an unforgiving posterity has indicted Calvin for a crime against humanity. Counsel for the defence would want it to be recorded that he pleaded with the council, unsuccessfully, for Servetus to be beheaded rather than incinerated.

How had Calvin done it? How was it that by 1553 the civil magistracy was even more zealous than Calvin himself in its determination to 'live by the Gospel'? The simple answer lies in his command of the pulpit: Geneva was preached into submission to the will of God. It was an unrelenting onslaught on its ears. There were daily sermons, three on Sundays. Calvin's contribution was 260 sermons a year, conceived lying in bed and delivered without notes. So perhaps this was creeping theocracy after all. Muslim clerics attempt less with their weekly sermons at Friday prayers.

But if Calvin had no wish to see his sermons enshrined in print (shorthand writers took them down for the benefit of refugees whose French was limited), he was a writer on a grand scale. Like Bullinger in Zürich, he never stopped writing letters. If Luther made the fortunes of the Wittenberg printers, Calvin made Geneva a major centre of protestant publishing. The city even acquired a new industry, paper-making. Between 1550 and 1560, 130 refugee printers and booksellers settled in Geneva, among them two famous names, Jean Crespin and, above all, a prince of the book trade, the Parisian Robert Estienne. The output rose from 137 titles in the 1540s to 527 between 1551 and 1564.

Calvin published as much in French as in Latin, since his gaze was always on the fortunes of the Reformation in his native land, and in some of the Latin works he was a self-appointed and effective spokesman for the cause of the Reformation more generally. Yet Calvin can be regarded as the author of one book, or at least of a book that outweighed everything else, his *Institutes*, and it is time to investigate what kind of book it was, its architecture as well as content. *Institutio* meant 'instruction' and it was originally a kind of catechism, a modest six chapters in the first edition of 1536, but also a manifesto, which carried a dedication to King Francis I stating, 'This is what we are about.' The 1539 edition was longer, seventeen chapters. In the French editions Calvin let his hair down. The simple Latin *'illi'* becomes *'ces canailles'*, *'ces chiens matins'*, *'ces opiniatres'*. In its final versions (Latin 1559, French 1560) the *Institutes* became a veritable summa, eighty chapters disposed in four books, adapted to the structure of the Apostles' Creed.

The most prominent characteristic of the *Institutes* is its balance. It is a fundamental error to suppose that it is a book that teaches 'Calvinism' and that 'Calvinism' is the same thing as the doctrine of predestination. It is true that Calvin believed that God 'elected' those whom he intended should be saved. So did St Thomas Aquinas. It is also true that Calvin as pastor and preacher believed (along with other Calvinists) that this was a useful doctrine which should be taught and applied. However, it had no centrality in Calvin's achievement as a systematic theologian. Book One of the *Institutes* opens with God, 'What it is to know God'; Book Two deals with the knowledge of God in Christ; and Book Three with how we obtain salvation. Only when we reach Chapter Twenty-One of this third book (Chapter Fifty-Six of the whole) do we come to 'Of the Eternal Election, By Which God Has Predestinated Some To Salvation, And Others To Destruction', and it proves to be one of the shorter chapters, some five thousand words. In Book Four we move on to what might be called applied theology: Church, sacraments, discipline and, last but not least, civil government, a subject to which Calvin devoted fourteen thousand words. Magistrates (who included monarchs) were 'gods', so when

James I went on about the 'divine right of kings' he was not abandoning his Calvinism.

Calvin died in 1564. By then the tide of religious refugees was still moving towards an overcrowded Geneva, but it had also started to flow in the opposite direction as pastors and colporteurs (peddlers of little Geneva books intended for the semi-literate) began to go home, especially into France where the fields were white already to harvest (John 4:35) but the labourers few (Matthew 9:37). Eighty-eight pastors sent between 1555 and 1563 may seem a lot, but the rapid advance of the Reform had reached the stage of *églises dressées* (churches publicly if not legally 'established'), perhaps 1750 of them by 1570. In 1560 there may have been two million Protestants, ten per cent of the population, more than there would ever be again in French history. The percentage was much higher in the Midi. In the absence of pastors carrying the licence of Geneva congregations had to provide their own leadership. This was a worry for Calvin, who was as much interested in control as evangelism. In 1559 the first national synod of a French Reformed Church was held, underground, in Paris. It adopted a Confession of Faith and a Form of Discipline patented in Geneva. Calvin was invisibly in the chair. Structures of ministry and church government originally devised for a small city-state were being adapted to serve the needs of a church organized on a national scale.

Calvin may have lived and worked in a republic but he never ceased to hope that France as a whole, which meant its monarchy, would be converted to true religion. He did not want French Protestants to live pell mell, like rats in straw. Even when the repression of Protestants became fierce he never sanctioned armed resistance, to the desperate frustration of those on the receiving end, who looked for more than prayers and tears. Nor could he condone casual violence and outrages committed against religious objects and persons.

But that was how things were going as society polarized, exacerbated by the structural weakness of the French state. If the Reformation was predominantly an urban movement it also attracted the nobility (including, in English terms, the gentry) in disproportionate numbers, who were often drawn into the movement by their womenfolk. These Protestants were not looking for a quiet future as a tolerated nonconformist group meeting in some backstreet bethel. Their conventicles were ready to invade and take over the churches. The noisy singing of metrical psalms (Geneva culture) was assertive if not aggressive, more 'protest songs' than hymns.

For six summer nights in 1558 three to four thousand psalm-singing demonstrators occupied the Pré-aux-Clercs, a pleasant park on the left bank of the Seine in Paris. Members of the nobility naturally came to worship armed, since for men of their class a sword was like an umbrella and sometimes, so to speak, it rained. In the winter of 1561–2 there was much street violence, with atrocities committed on both sides. What was different about an event at Vassy in Champagne on 1 March was that the leading catholic prince, François de Guise, personally directed an attack on a protestant congregation meeting legally under an edict of toleration, albeit in a barn, killing about fifty worshippers. A month later Louis, Prince de Condé, leader of the Protestants, issued a declaration that began forty years of intermittent religious wars – eight in all, according to arithmetical historians.

A longer book than this would have space to anatomize the progress of Protestantism of a more or less Calvinist kind elsewhere in Europe: Scotland, the Netherlands, Hungary, the German principality of the Palatinate. Its impact was naturally different in every one of these diverse environments: revolution in Scotland of a traditional Scottish kind, turbulent and headed by the nobility; revolution in the Netherlands of a Netherlandish kind, popular and urban, a movement that would never have won more than ten per cent of the votes in a democratic election but which by the end of the sixteenth century had played an indispensable part in the creation of a new player on the European stage, the Dutch Republic. In Hungary, where the Reformed Church is to this day one of the four most substantial in Europe, a home-grown Calvinism that had little direct contact with Geneva played a quite different role, shoring up a nation-state under threat. In Germany Calvinism, like Lutheranism, was a princely thing ('court Calvinism'), dependent on the preferences, almost the whims, of its rulers. In the Rhenish Palatinate the elector, Frederick III, introduced Calvinism which, with a brief Lutheran interlude between 1576 and 1583, remained the religion of the state until the 1620s. His seat, Heidelberg, became a centre of Calvinist learning and theology second only in importance to Geneva itself, and it was the source of one of the most authoritative of Calvinist confessions of faith, the Heidelberg Catechism. In all these cases, the brand mark of Calvinism was an inner-worldly religious activism that contrasts with the passivity of Lutheranism. This holds true even for the princely Reformation in the Palatinate, which was the most militant of German states, a little Prussia out of its time – until the Counter-Reformation caught up with it.

So Calvinism was an international movement. To deal with its history as a series of national histories is to miss much of the point about its internationalism. Calvinist Protestants had a creed and a cause that transcended frontiers, and which was manifested not just through their political sympathies but through their pockets and purses. English Calvinists intervened militarily in Scotland, in the first War of Religion in France, and in the Netherlands. They welcomed and helped to sustain churches of French and Dutch 'strangers' in London and other places. They raised money for the defence of Geneva against the duke of Savoy in the 1580s and for the relief of the Palatinate, devastated by the Thirty Years' War, in the 1620s. This is a story about soldiers (volunteers or mercenaries) and financiers.

We are nearly at the end of a chapter on Calvinism in which we have yet to define Calvinism. Like almost all religious signifiers, it originated as a term of abuse, in the late 1550s, a time of defining conflict between the hardline Lutherans of north German cities such as Hamburg and the cities of the Germanic south, which was fought out especially in the small churches of displaced protestant refugees that were to be found in many of these towns. The problem was not only the Eucharist, although it included that. Calvin, it has been argued, was not himself a Calvinist, and books have been written on the theme of 'Calvin Against the Calvinists'.

Too much has been made of that. What Calvinism became was in a consistent sequence with what John Calvin preached, wrote and did. As a system of thought and practice, however, it was the creation of the next generation and especially of Théodore de Bèze (1519–1605), known as Beza, the first professor of the Geneva Academy, where he taught for almost forty years. Beza became Calvin's successor as first in rank in the Company of Pastors and a counsellor to churches and civil governments who enjoyed international status. It was Beza who for all those years saved Calvinism from the internecine disputes that tore Lutheranism apart after the death of Luther. His style was to crystallize and harden. Predestination was hardened, becoming a divine decree that actually preceded the fall of Adam and even the Creation itself, so-called supralapsarian predestination. The Calvinist church order was now held to be universally normative, even in monarchical states, and a letter from Beza on the subject of bishops helped to launch Presbyterianism in England and Scotland (although even Beza knew how to apply the soft pedal when he wrote to Elizabeth of England). Calvinist politics were stiffened and Beza sanctioned, as Calvin never had, the right of 'inferior magistrates' to resist tyrannical rulers.

These were incidentals. More fundamentally, Beza and the Heidelberg theologians have been credited with turning Calvinist divinity into a new kind of scholasticism, a system of propositions to be asserted, attacked and defended with the weapons of dialectic and much dependent on proof-texts, some of which were employed to prove Presbyterianism. This was a departure from the theological method of Calvin's Christian humanism. In the future there were to be fierce contentions in the universities and academies of Calvinist Europe, not least in the Netherlands, where the anti-predestinarian doctrine of Jacobus Arminius (1560–1609) divided the Dutch Republic and contributed to the fall and execution of its greatest statesman, Johan van Oldenbarnevelt.

That is doubtless too negative a note on which to end this brief sketch of the origins and early development of Calvinism. In Scotland, in seventeenth-century England, and not least in those parts of North America now to be christened New England, it contributed its immense creative as well as disruptive influence to political and social life. Some historians and social theorists have credited Calvinism with the invention of modern politics and even of something called 'the spirit of capitalism', if not capitalism itself. We shall come back to these ambitious claims in the final chapter.

7 Counter-Reformation

A German book on the subject has the title *Katholische Reformation oder Gegenreformation?* (Catholic Reformation or Counter-Reformation?). 'Counter-Reformation' implies a reaction, 'Catholic Reformation' a spring of renewal gushing of its own accord out of the rock of the Church. An English historian has neatly untied this Gordian knot: 'Was it not quite obviously both?'

But the German historian's question is not meaningless. In 1543 a little book was published in Venice with the title *Trattato utilissimo del beneficio di Giesu Christo crocifisso i christiani* (A Most Useful Treatise on the Merits of Jesus Christ Crucified for Christians), written by an elusive Benedictine monk called Benedetto da Mantova (dates of birth and death unknown, but his surname seems to have been Fontanino) with some help from the humanist and poet Marcantonio Flaminio (1498–1550), a popular work of piety that was translated into several languages including Croat. At first sight this may appear to be a piece of native Italian Christocentrism, part of a Pauline and Augustinian renaissance known to have been nourished by a Spanish humanist and biblicist, Juan de Valdés (1500–41), whose pious circle in Naples had included Flaminio. But the *Beneficio* can be read in more than one way. It proves to have been made up from a number of transalpine protestant texts, and especially the 1539 edition of Calvin's *Institutes*. Whether or not Benedetto had come across Calvin in his monastery on the slopes of Mount Etna, which seems unlikely, the *Institutes* was known to Flaminio.

It is hard to distinguish between the theology of the *Beneficio* and Protestantism. 'Man can never do good works unless he first know himself to be justified by faith.' Other scholars insist, however, that the *Beneficio* is an expression of Evangelism, a movement that was not generated by Protestantism and should be distinguished from it. What is certain is that the *Beneficio* was presently placed on the Index and so successfully repressed by the Roman Inquisition that of the many thousands of copies of the Italian edition that were once in existence only one is known to survive, discovered in the library of a Cambridge college in the nineteenth century. That sort of successful repression was Counter-Reformation.

There are two ways of containing and controlling such a vast and unruly subject. One method uses building blocks: the Spanish and Italian proto-reformers; new religious orders, especially the Jesuits; the reactive watershed of the Roman Inquisition (1542) and the Index of Prohibited Books (1559); the Council of Trent; the Counter-Reformation popes; the mission to recover Christendom for the Church in Germany and, through the heroic self-giving of martyr priests, in Elizabethan England, and to extend it by means of new conquests for Christ in the Americas, Japan and China; the politics of the Counter-Reformation, which included the troops sent along the Spanish Road to the Netherlands, the Spanish Armada, and the suppression of the Reformation in Bohemia, Silesia and the Palatinate; Counter-Reformation aesthetics (mannerist painting, Titian and Rubens, the music of Palestrina and Lassus); the saints of the Counter-Reformation (St Teresa of Avila, St John of the Cross); and, born out of time and rather late, the grandeur of the Counter-Reformation in seventeenth-century France, its many schools of devotion, its controversies and its writers (Pascal, Bossuet, Fénelon). By this time the reader, like the author, will be in need of a rest.

The other approach is to attempt to capture the 'spirit' of the Counter-Reformation, to extract its essence. If the first approach is tedious and threatens to turn into a dense catalogue of names, the second, while more seductive, may be short on facts. We shall come eventually to the second, after a reconnaissance of some parts of the landscape mapped out in the first.

The Counter-Reformation was primary in Spain and Italy, secondary north of the Alps. According to some (especially German protestant historians), it all began in the Spain that had conquered Muslim Granada and was still ingesting half-converted Moors and Jews, a Spain dominated ecclesiastically by one of the most comprehensive reformers of the age, Cardinal Jiménez de Cisneros (1436–1517). Here repression and renewal went hand in hand. St Ignatius Loyola, the converted Basque soldier whose destiny was to found the Society of Jesus, came out of this mould, although his spirituality was not purely Spanish but owed a debt to the New Devotionist tradition in the Low Countries. There were also Netherlandish elements in the mystical, millenarian and sometimes erotic movement of the *Alumbrados* (in Latin *Illuminati*), which attracted the attention of the Spanish Inquisition in hundreds of prosecutions – which is why so much is known about it. There is less to know about 'orthodox' Spanish Protestantism, which was strangled at birth. The political Counter-Reformation which committed itself to the extirpation of heresy would be seen as a Spanish thing from the viewpoints of Paris, Leiden, London and as far away as Jamestown, Virginia.

In Italy, Catholic Reformation preceded Counter-Reformation and in more favourable political circumstances might have matured into a variant form of Protestant Reformation. The free republic of Lucca was on the brink of responding to the stirring evangelism of the crypto-Protestant Pietro Martire Vermigli (1499–1562) as if it were a Swiss or south German city. But the Roman Inquisition, in the first year of its operations, forced Peter Martyr to pull off his mask, or at least to consider his position, and with other leaders of what was now an abortive reformation to go into exile north of the Alps. Under these circumstances Italian Protestantism developed eclectic tendencies. The engineer Jacobus Acontius (c.1520–67) settled in Elizabethan England, where he became the most outspoken apologist for religious toleration that the age produced; while Lelio Sozzini (1525–62) and his nephew Fausto (1539–1604), both natives of Siena, travelled as far as Poland to find a reception for their pioneering anti-Trinitarian views (Socinianism).

The Italian Reformation was a child of the Renaissance, of the audaciously critical biblical humanism of Valla, which helped to inspire the Neoplatonizing Florentines Marsilio Ficino (1433–99) and Pico della Mirandola (1463–94) and formed the mind of the Englishman John Colet (1467–1519). The University of Padua was a crucible for a kind of intellectual idealism and many of the reformers were its alumni, including another Englishman, Reginald Pole (1500–58), who was to have a prominent role at the Council of Trent. The Counter-Reformation, however, also came out of the anti-Renaissance of the holocaust of 'vanities' that accompanied the millennial regime in Florence of the severe Dominican Girolamo Savonarola (1452–1498). Savonarola left a deep impression. Although he was born in Florence seventeen years after Savonarola had been burned at the stake, St Philip Neri (1515–95), the most attractive of Counter-Reformation saints, called the 'Apostle of

Rome' but never more than a simple priest, was a kind of disciple. The Venetian patrician Gasparo Contarini (1483–1542) was equally impressed. On Holy Saturday 1511 (another conversion watershed – 'I was changed from great fear and suffering to happiness') he became convinced that a Christian is justified by faith rather than works, a little before Luther got there.

Contarini, a statesman and prince of the Church, did not pursue the doctrine into its Lutheran implications, but as long as he lived and had influence and allies among the 'spirituali' (especially Pole) a consensual doctrine of justification was a possibility. At a summit in Regensburg in 1541 agreement was reached with Melanchthon, Bucer and other Protestants. 'It is a secure and wholesome teaching that the sinner is justified by a living and effectual faith.' But Regensburg was repudiated by the pope and at Trent. A year later and Contarini was dead. It was 1542, the year that launched the Inquisition and expelled Italy's would-be reformers, the moment when, in a conventional perspective, Catholic Reformation turned into Counter-Reformation.

The year 1527 had an impact like that of 11 September 2001. In that year Rome, which had backed the French horse in the latest stages of the Italian Wars, was sacked (the word fails to convey the atrocious enormity of the event) by mutinous imperial troops. The *Gravamina* of the German nation had come home to roost. The world would not be the same again. Gianmatteo Giberti (1495–1543), a failed politician who had been the most powerful person in the Curia but whose diplomacy had been largely responsible for the debacle of 1527, left Rome to reside in his diocese of Verona, which he proceeded to reform with a series of episcopal visitations. This was a landmark and a signal that the reform of the Church was, against all expectations, to be undertaken by the bishops. Giberti's example was to be followed, most famously by St Carlo Borromeo (1538–84), archbishop of Milan (from 1565), with synods, councils, visitations, the reform of everything in sight from funerals to clerical dress and church furnishings.

The new religious seriousness found fulfilment in new religious orders. In 1524 the Theatines – named for the diocesan style of one of their founders, the Neapolitan Gian Pietro Carafa (1476–1559), the mastermind of the reaction of 1542 and subsequently the fiercest of Counter-Reformation popes – were born out of the Roman Oratory of Divine Love, one of several such sodalities in Italian cities dating from about 1500. Living in community but active in the world, the Theatines ministered to the poor and the sick, especially to syphilitics, the AIDS suffers of the time. A direct line runs to the Jesuits, founded in 1540 by the papal bull *Regimini militantis ecclesiae*, with their dedication, at first only vaguely defined, 'to the progress of souls in Christian life and doctrine and to the propagation of the faith'. Second in importance only to the Jesuits were the reformed Franciscans known as Capuchins. Founded in 1528, within a hundred years they had almost twenty thousand members in 1260 houses in forty-two provinces. A little later came St Philip Neri's Congregation of the Oratory.

By the 1530s even the supreme pontiff knew that the Church was in crisis. Paul III (1534–49) was an unlikely reformer, an old-fashioned nepotist who as a cardinal had had a mistress who bore him four children, and who had built the luxurious Palazzo Farnese and delighted Rome with fireworks and a souped-up carnival. But in 1536 Paul appointed 'a Select Commission of Cardinals and Other Prelates Concerning the Reform of the Church', which included the spirituali Contarini, Carafa,

Giberti and Pole. These were all his appointees to the Sacred College, more evidence of his seriousness. Their report, the *Consilium de Emendanda Ecclesia* (1537), was in the tradition of reform packages but more radical than most. For example, it recommended the dissolution of all but the strictest religious orders. The central proposition that Rome must first reform itself, on the principle of *purga Romam, purgator mundus*, echoed the German *Gravamina*. It is not often physicians themselves who say, 'Physician, heal thyself.'

The *Consilium*, like the reports that come out of royal commissions, gathered dust. The Curia, which had no representation on the commission, saw to that. It was leaked to the press and a German translation appeared with a cartoon showing foxes sweeping a room with their own tails. But it was a start, and was intended to prepare the way for the General Council that the crisis had long demanded, a plough to which Paul III had put his hand at the time of his election.

Intentions were one thing, achievement quite another. A credible Council needed the participation of both the Habsburgs and the French, who were usually at war, and a Council capable of healing the schism would need to secure the attendance of the German Protestants. The emperor, Charles V, and his brother and designated successor, Ferdinand, king of Hungary and Bohemia, were not interested in anything less. There were abortive meetings at Mantua (1537) and Vicenza (1539), and a desperate attempt to square the circle of doctrinal disagreement at Regensburg (1541), followed by the Carafan reaction of 1542, which was a programme of (repressive) reform without a Council, and then another miscarriage, at Trent itself (1543).

So it was a weary diplomatic triumph when the nineteenth General Council at last met. But it was a generation too late, the result of what the modern historian of the Council has called 'a calamitous concatenation of circumstances'. The place was the little Alpine city of Trent, a Germanic sort of place (its bishops were always Germans) lying deep in the valley of the Adige as you travel down from the Brenner Pass into Italy. The Council was good news for the property owners of Trent, who could charge as much as they liked for accommodation. The protestant historian Sleidan, part of the press corps, was astonished to find that he had to pay twelve florins a week for two rooms and two meals a day.

This was not the Council the situation demanded. Not only were there no Protestants at Trent, only one German bishop turned up and most of the rest (all twenty-five of them) were Italian. It was December 1545, nine months after the papal legates had first arrived in Trent to inaugurate the Council, nine months given up to serpentine politics. The first phase of the Council ran until March 1547 when Paul III killed it stone dead by transferring it to Bologna in the Papal States. That meant that when Charles V defeated the protestant princes in the Schmalkaldic War there was no Council to which he could frog-march the vanquished. The Council reassembled at Trent in May 1551, but the expected protestant participation never materialized and the French were forbidden by their king to attend. The pope from 1550–55 was Julius III, a sick joke who made a young 'nephew' (toyboy?) a cardinal; and after the twenty-two days of Marcellus (memorable as pope only for the mass that Palestrina wrote for his funeral) came the election of Carafa as Pope Paul IV (1555–9). Trent would remain off the agenda as long as he lived. It reconvened in 1561 for the best attended and most fruitful of its assemblies. It was now the French, facing religious war, who had the greatest interest in making something of it. When the Council finally dispersed in November 1563 it left behind a bundle of decrees that defined much of the Catholicism of the next four centuries, in bulk more legislation than had been generated by all previous eighteen General Councils of the Church together. A nest of mice having laboured gave birth to a mountain.

A General Council might have been an occasion for the two sides of the religious divide to explain to each other what their words meant – 'ecumenical' in our modern sense. Instead, what Trent did was to restate what Catholics believed in terms that bore the same relation to Protestantism as does a negative to a photographic print. On 13 January 1547 the Council declared its mind, after much heart-searching, on the matter of justification: a decree of sixteen chapters with thirty-three canons attached. Canon 9 reads: 'If anyone saith that by faith alone the impious is justified . . . let him be anathema.' It was entirely due to Luther that Catholicism was now defined in relation to that doctrine! Trent reorganized the Church in ways that made it not only a credible instrument of Christian formation and pastoral care but waterproof against protestant error, a Church with a siege mentality.

In the second place, a General Council might have been expected to cut the overweening Renaissance papacy down to size, to make the Church conciliar, which had been the promise (or threat) of Constance and Basle. That was one principal reason why it took so long for Rome to decide that a Council would be a good idea at all, and for the Church at large to be convinced that any pope was capable of convening a Council worthy of the name. In the event, however, Trent became an instrument of papal aggrandizement. If there was to be reform of the drastic kind outlined in the *Consilium*, let it be top-down, transmitted from Rome through bishops and nuncios. This was achieved because the Council was held in Italy; because ecclesiastical geography determined that there would be a massive over-representation of Italy at any assembly constituted primarily of bishops and in which (unlike Basle and Constance) only bishops were permitted to vote; and because the papal legates guiding Trent along its tortuous road proved to be good at management.

One critical decision at Trent was a compromise. Some, including the emperor, wanted the Council to concern itself with the reform of abuses, the old German programme and one that had some chance of attracting 'heretics' back into a big tent, especially if 'abuses' were extended to include clerical celibacy and the withholding of the cup from the laity at Communion. But the papal interest lay in the erection of a doctrinal ring-fence. What happened, although this was never formalized, was that issues of reform and doctrinal definition proceeded *pari passu* and alternately.

The early sessions of the Council came to universally conservative decisions about matters of contested doctrine, which is to say that the Council confirmed Catholic Reformation as Counter-Reformation. The decree on justification, the doctrinal masterpiece of the Council, rejected not only Lutheranism but the eirenic doctrine of so-called 'double justification' (sanctification coupled with justification) accepted at Regensburg and advanced at Trent by Cardinal Giralomo Seripando (1493–1563), general of the Augustinian order. The fourth session ruled that saving truth is to be found not only in the Bible (the protestant *sola scriptura*) but in the unwritten traditions of the Church. The old Latin Vulgate version of the Bible was declared to be 'authentic', and the bishops were henceforth to control the publication of bibles and commentaries. The Council offered little encouragement to those who wanted to replace the scholastic exploration of scripture with biblical humanism. Counter-Reformation seminaries would be bastions of a reinforced scholasticism. St Thomas Aquinas had not, after all, outlived his sell-by date.

It was the third session of the Council that did most to refashion the practice of Catholicism and its supporting structures, the essence of Tridentine reform. The bishops were to be its instruments, the equivalent of what are called line managers in the modern business world. The procedures for their appointment strictly regulated, they were to hold annual synods and visitations, which would reveal whatever might be amiss, a new ideal of the bishop as pastor, to be realized to the utmost in the Milan of Borromeo. But what were bishops: representatives of Christ on earth in their own (divine) right, or mere subalterns of Christ's only vicar on earth, the pope? That was the fiercest debate in this third period. A powerful Spanish contingent argued for the first of these positions which, if adopted, would have meant that the pope could not withdraw a bishop from the duty of episcopal residence in order to staff his Curia. Since Trent was in any case to empower the Tridentine episcopate this debate may seem academic, part of the detritus of history. But it would be renewed, four centuries later almost to the year, when the Second Vatican Council rediscovered episcopal collegiality as a principle on which the well-being of the Church depends, albeit one to which Pope John Paul II has attached rather less importance.

If it was important that Trent put the Church under episcopal command, subject to papal high command, it was more important still that it created a Church run at the grassroots by priests, and priests who were now to be formed, almost manufactured, according to the Tridentine pattern-book. That was implicit in a decree of the twenty-third session that every diocese should have its own seminary, which would be subject to uniform regulations, the seminarians to wear the tonsure and clerical dress and to be instructed in the administration of the sacraments, 'especially those things which shall seem adapted to enable them to hear confessions'. This was the Church of the next four centuries in embryo, the Church of the humble cleric Jean-Baptiste Marie Vianney (1786–1859), known universally as the Curé d'Ars, canonized in 1925 and made the patron of all parish priests. The medieval Church had never been, in this sense and to this degree, clerical.

Now came the age of a reformed and reinvigorated papacy. Pius IV (1559–65), who had reconvened Trent, made a start. However, it was Pius V (1566–72), the first pope to be canonized for a very long time, former shepherd boy and professional inquisitor, who demonstrated what the office was capable of. A universal enforcer, rigorous against not only heresy (he told his troops, intervening in the French religious wars, to take no prisoners) but also Jews, homosexuals and matadors (he prohibited bullfights), Pius was a political pope, the last in history to depose a reigning sovereign (Elizabeth I of England, in the 1570 bull *Regnans in excelsis*). This helped form the English perception of 'popery' as not only false religion but diabolical politics. Gregory XIII (1572–85) was more ordinary, and worldly, but he was the pope who ordered a solemn Te Deum to celebrate the Massacre of St Bartholomew (1572). His successor Sixtus V (1585–90) may have been pope for only five years, but those five years recreated Rome as Europe's greatest city, the centre of a new economy, and the seat of an effective and modernizing government. The first was achieved by means of a new, star-shaped city plan, the streets, piazzas, fountains and obelisks that are the Rome of modern tourism (requiring only Bernini to ice the cake); the second by creating governmental ministries ('congregations' of this and that), which have administered the Catholic Church ever since. One of these, the Congregation of the Council, was designed to enforce Trent.

In all of these efforts the new papacy's right arm was the Society of Jesus. Jesuit theologians won the debate with the Spanish episcopalians at Trent, ran the new seminaries all over Europe, infiltrated royal courts and universities, and were indefatigable preachers, great missionaries and formidable polemicists. The Dutchman Peter Canisius (1521–97) presided over the recovery and consolidation of Catholicism in south Germany and Austria, where there were a dozen Jesuit colleges, and wrote catechisms designed for every age group and intellectual capacity. The entry of two Jesuit fathers, Edmund Campion (1540–81) and Robert Parsons (1546–1610) into Elizabethan England in 1580 prompted a usually restrained historian to term the event an invasion.

It is a cliché to call the Jesuits the shock troops of the papacy, and, like most clichés, it is true. But here lies a paradox, even a contradiction, and to penetrate it is to encounter questions about the relation of freedom to authority in all human systems. Jesuits could be rebels, and have been in our own time. That was always a potential in their spiritual formation and their constitution. Every Jesuit, and the thousands of lay devotees who enrolled themselves in the Jesuit spiritual gym, went through the *Spiritual Exercises*, a distillation of what St Ignatius had experienced in a cave at Manresa, near Barcelona, and a kind of manual for soul maintenance. The *Exercises* provided a total exposure to Christ of an autonomous human being – in the words of its title, a means 'to conquer oneself and order one's life'. Jesuit theologians would always uphold the freedom of the will, especially in their struggle with the

Jansenists (the Calvinists of the Counter-Reformation) in seventeenth-century France.

There was also a fundamental principle of freedom embodied in the Jesuit Constitutions, which may on the face of it appear to be all about discipline. It is a uniquely flexible document that allows for enterprise and informality in procuring the *majorem gloriam Dei*, while requiring a nearly absolute obedience to the general and the rest of the high command, and ultimately to the pope. A modern military analogue might be the SAS, where initiative is as much at a premium as discipline. And if religion for the Jesuits was warfare it was also business, *negotium*, and it was the expanding trade routes and quickening commercial activity of the sixteenth century that made possible the explosion of the Jesuits across Europe and beyond. Communication by letter, a speciality of the Society, held the order together, but, since they took weeks or even months to reach their destinations, letters were as much about enterprise and autonomy as about reporting to headquarters. Conditions in a German college, or an Elizabethan priest's hole, or a Brazilian jungle, or in Japan were very various and were variously reported.

Virginia Woolf described George Eliot's *Middlemarch* as the first novel written for grown-ups. We might say something similar of a book on the Counter-Reformation published, posthumously, in 1968, the first reflective investigation of the subject in English. H. Outram Evennett's *The Spirit of the Counter-Reformation* is a clearing in the forest after those dense thickets of events, names and dates. What, according to Evennett, was the Counter-Reformation's essential spirit? It was not to be found in the Council of Trent, for Evennett believed that 'spiritual rebirth and enlightenment . . . are not achieved at ecumenical councils'. It was what he called 'the evolutionary adaptation of the Catholic religion and of the Catholic Church to new forces both in the spiritual and in the material order'. It 'ensured the survival into the post-medieval world of a still-persuasive, still-expanding, world form of Christianity under a single centralised control.' That applied even to the Counter-Reformation papacy, for those popes were doing for a new sort of Church what the so-called 'new monarchies' were doing for states. But the 'spirit' was not to be found in ecclesiastical state-building but in spirituality, and naturally the Society of Jesus was what Evennett's Counter-Reformation was very largely about. Ignatius, too, was not fighting but embracing the general tendencies of his age. He was part of the great age of discovery.

In bringing Evennett to press, John Bossy suggested that in order for his claims to be fully substantiated he ought to have paid more attention to what happened to the Counter-Reformation next. Evennett had written of 'a point of repose' by the third quarter of the seventeenth century. Bossy thought that a polite word for a principle of morbidity. In making a special study of English Catholicism in the period, Bossy contrasted the spiritually adventurous activism of the Jesuits with inbuilt forces of inertia and concluded that inertia won out. More generally, Bossy granted that 'the petering out of the Counter-Reformation' was, in part, the consequence of a crisis in Mediterranean civilization, a shift of the centre of gravity to an Atlantic world that was to be predominantly Protestant. The Counter-Reformation was a Latin invention, not very adaptable north of the Alps. But why was that? Bossy is clearly sceptical about Evennett's modernizing Counter-Reformation. And by the mid-seventeenth century 'the moment would seem to have passed when Catholicism could have established itself at any depth in the heart of the rising civilisation of northern Europe.'

A hundred and fifty years of 'crippling immobility' were to ensue. Protestants and post-Protestants can only nod in agreement. They will want to remember Galileo and his response when the Inquisition condemned his circling planets: 'Eppur si muove' ('But it does move all the same'), a remark to set alongside 'Here I stand', especially since Galileo did not actually say it.

In a more recent book (*Peace in the Post-Reformation*) Bossy has proposed the broadest possible comparison of the Catholicism of the Counter-Reformation with what had preceded it. His premiss is that religion was, or had been, almost primarily a mechanism for peace-making. Medieval communities could not afford the luxury of feuding and fighting, and the Church and its professional functionaries were there to prevent conflict. The sacraments, which professed to be about man and God, were also, and in popular perception even mainly, social institutions. This was the 'moral tradition'. However, in the exemplary episcopate of St Carlo Borromeo, enforcement of religious observance took over from the regulation of social behaviour and references to *pax* almost disappeared from the liturgy. The Borromeoan symbol of the new Catholicism was the confessional-box with its grille, its invisibility, the instrument of an unsocial idea of sin and forgiveness: the parishioner and his priest, man and his God. In late sixteenth-century Germany the moral tradition was alive and well, among the Lutherans. The Jesuits were a machine for its impoverishment and the extinction of the Lutheran achievement in maintaining it.

Bossy's Borromeo wished to get to grips with real life but failed to do so. Naturally this was some sort of victory for real life, which is always likely to win in the end. The Counter-Reformation in Italy in its sterner manifestations was a bushfire, and after it the landscape recovered. Peace-making was not extinguished. But the half-spoken implication is that in the partial abandonment by the official Church of the moral tradition lies the reason for the ultimate failure of the Counter-Reformation, and perhaps of Catholicism itself, which is now becoming apparent after what looks like the artificial boost given to its fortunes by the nineteenth century. Yet Protestants are not invited to crow. What they provided in place of the moral tradition has had even less ultimate staying power. Civil society, sceptical and rational, secular and material in its aspirations and at odds with Christian society, is the real terminus of the moral tradition. For how long it can remain civil without being Christian is a question that, fortunately, the historian cannot be expected to ask, let alone answer.

I am not sure that we ought to leave the argument there. John Bossy is one of those historians who is never less than brilliant but whom many of his peers often find (or claim) to have been wrong. Against his morbid analysis of the long-term fortunes of Counter-Reformation Catholicism one could argue that this new Catholicism was part of the expansion of European civilization in the seventeenth and eighteenth centuries, that it contained its own Enlightenment. This could be maintained with reference to the aesthetics of the Baroque, to education, to social welfare, not least in France. Modern Ireland, for better or worse, may now be outgrowing its Catholic past. Yet what made modern Ireland but the Catholic Church?

8 *Exceptional cases: the Reformation in the British Isles*

The English Reformation, and indeed the Reformation in all parts of the British Isles, was exceptional in the extent to which it was contested, both at the time and ever since. The history of religious change in the sixteenth century was different in England, Wales, Scotland and Ireland. In the seventeenth century, however, when for the first time all parts of these islands were subject to the same monarch, their religion and politics were a history of interactions, so that no sense can be made of one case without reference to all the others.

Ireland had its English problem and so had Scotland. England might have been better off without either. In England the Reformation was made by the monarchy; in Scotland its inception and forward progress were for much of the time anti-monarchical. Those ignorant of history but informed about the present may be surprised to learn that there was an Irish Reformation at all, as distinct from the immigration of Scottish Protestants from across the Northern Channel into Ulster. There was, although it was not a great success, and why that should have been so has launched a raft of books. Wales may appear to have been a relatively quiet and uncomplicated case, borrowing its Reformation from England and merely turning it into Welsh – until we discover that it had its real Reformation in later centuries, even as late as the revival of 1904 when all those gaunt chapels calling themselves Bethel and Zoar came to punctuate the landscape, destined within a hundred years to become carpet warehouses and bingo halls, leaving behind no religion beyond choirs and rugby.

So to England. There is a myth about the English Reformation and the myth is that it never happened. Many Anglicans would once have had you believe that it consisted of little more than a few moderate and sensible adjustments to a Church of England that had no need of the ructions happening on something called The Continent and which was exceptionally conscious of its continuity with the past. That is indeed a mythical history which serves its non-historical purpose. Looked at from a considerable distance, the working out of an English Reformation that was in fact drastic was a dialectic involving the most effective, if by no means most powerful, monarchy in Europe, which expected to be obeyed and for the most part was, and a nation that for all its regional and local variety was cohesive and already constituted some kind of civil society. It was aware, too, that it was a nation, although that awareness was enhanced by the very processes we are discussing. The key to what happened was the common law of England, which determined that what the royal government ordered by way of religious change was for the most part carried out, however unpopular it may have been. We need look no further for an explanation of how it was that English Protestants and Catholics, unlike their French counterparts, were not given to slaughtering each other in the streets.

Attempts at understanding how the dialectic worked can lead to misunderstanding, especially when historical bias leads to the overemphasis of one side or the other of the equation. The Tudor monarchy was strong but it was not, as was once thought, some kind of despotism. So can we say that in throwing its disproportionate weight behind the forces making for religious change it was responding to a popular mood, the mood at least of the ruling class, even sensing the manifest destiny of the country it ruled? Historians who on the whole have thought Protestantism a superior kind of religion, and one which was a suitable vehicle for the journey that England was about to undertake, have persuaded themselves that it was indeed an idea whose moment had arrived.

However, from most parts of England there is little evidence to support this view. 'Revisionists' have persuaded us that what happened in the Reformation was that one of the most Catholic of European countries in terms of its investment (literally) in the old religion became, within three generations, one of the most anti-Catholic. The death of the old religion was one of those strange deaths, unnatural wastage. Not that the religion was all that old: in many places before the decades of change, local communities and their rich benefactors, often working together, had enlarged their churches, erecting ambitious towers and spires and adding handsome church porches, which is where weddings took place. The images, painted panels, crosses and other ornaments that were about to be smashed or melted down were often brand new and brightly painted. If in the living experience of a man aged no more than fifty in 1570 it was a case of Philip Larkin's 'England's gone', it was not the faded England of what another poet, Browning, called 'that dear middle-age' but the England into which he had been born.

The idea that the English Reformation was a naked imposition will not work either. Some of the things that happened were not unpopular. After his fall from grace no one seems to have shed many tears for Cardinal Thomas Wolsey (1472/ 4–1530), the builder of Hampton Court, last and most overblown of the old-style prelates and Henry VIII's first minister. Nor were the other bishops much liked, although they were not powerful enough to attract the hatred and violence visited on some of the prince-bishops of Germany. The dissolution of the monasteries brought out onto the streets not protesters but opportunists who were eager to buy up monastic lands and to use the buildings as quarries, so that Catholic historians have written of a corrupt complicity in this tragedy. (The exception was in the north of England where monasteries were still relevant to a whole way of life, so that the dissolution helped to provoke the most threatening of the Tudor rebellions, the Pilgrimage of Grace of 1536-7.) The clergy were subject to criticism – they usually are – but often from fellow priests such as John Colet, dean of St Paul's, who had accompanied Erasmus to Walsingham and who in a tirade delivered to a synod held in 1510 lambasted their 'evil life', 'lust of the flesh', 'covetousness', the perennial complaints of reformers. Something called 'anticlericalism' was once proposed as the reason for the Reformation, but evidence that the clergy were detested as a caste is unreliable and the very word 'anticlericalism' is an anachronistic import from much more modern European politics.

The last generation of Catholic Englishmen believed that their dead grandparents and children were in purgatory and that prayers and masses could be efficacious in winning them remission. The evidence is in the hundreds of chantries founded by the rich and the many thousands of guilds and fraternities ('poor men's chantries') to which 'everyone' paid their subscriptions, their main function being the perpetuation of what has been called a religion celebrated by the living on behalf of the dead. So how was it that a government whose instruments of forcible coercion were limited was able, in a short space of time, to make such associations illegal and to confiscate many of their assets? This has been called the 'riddle of compliance'.

We may be forced to construct the following syllogism: a religious change so drastic and so unwelcome cannot have happened; but it did happen; ergo, it cannot have been all that drastic and unwelcome. Among those who believe that there was a great change, there is a consensus that it must be understood in terms of the interplay of what have been called 'from above' and 'from below' factors and forces. Neither top-down nor bottom-up explanations will work on their own. The history of the English Bible provides a good illustration of the double process. The Bible was translated by self-appointed volunteers, beginning with William Tyndale. This was reformation not only from below but from outside, since Tyndale worked in exile. The printers and booksellers naturally had their own interests in the project. Soon, however, Henry VIII adopted the Bible as a symbol and instrument of his majesty and it was placed, by order, in all churches.

There was no symmetry or perfect match in this process. Not even Henry VIII could control what all those people might make of scripture. The English Reformation in its secondary and tertiary developments produced a variety of dissenting nonconformities and a long-term future of religious pluralism. It was another of history's jokes that the first of these nonconformities should be the Catholicism that survived the Reformation as a repressed and disadvantaged minority, 'the popish sect' as Protestants disdainfully called it, until in the nineteenth century Irish immigration and papal ultramontanism made it something more than that.

If there might have been no Reformation without Luther, we can be rather more certain that the English Reformation, as a national event, would not have happened without Henry VIII. There was a long-standing heretical tradition in England, and once the Lollards started reading Tyndale's New Testament and other imported Lutheran books they began to reinvent themselves as a sectarian protestant church, with some inspiration and guidance from academics and clerics converted to the new opinions. Shall we hazard a guess and say that the result might have accounted for perhaps two per cent of the population, many more in London, the south-east and East Anglia than elsewhere? Grassroots Protestantism in France was soon much stronger than that, but that was because it attracted the patronage of the landowners, who in England would surely not have become Protestants in substantial numbers without encouragement from the top. We can make the event even more contingent: no Reformation if Henry's first wife, Catherine of Aragon, had borne him several healthy sons, or even just one. Henry's need to be released from a marriage that could not provide him with a male heir was the cause, or at least the occasion, of a religious revolution so closely tied up with personal and dynastic interest that the history books call it the Henrician Reformation.

This, and only this, was why a series of Acts of Parliament between 1531 and 1534 severed the English Church from the Roman obedience and subjected its bishops and other clergy to total dependence on the Crown, a legal isolation from the remainder of Christendom. The process, which was masterminded by Thomas Cromwell, who had stepped into Wolsey's ministerial shoes, was summed up in the statute that proclaimed that 'this realm of England is an empire', or in modern language a fully sovereign state, 'governed by one supreme head and king'. The coping stone was the Act of Supremacy of 1534 which acknowledged and gave legal force to the claim of the king's majesty to be 'the only supreme head of the Church of England', with virtually unlimited powers to intervene in its affairs – as ever, in the name of reform: 'from time to time to visit, repress, redress, reform, order, correct, restrain and amend all such errors, heresies, abuses, offences . . .'

Revolutions acquire a momentum that is hard to stop. In the England of the 1530s religious revolution was pushed forward by Henry's new queen, Anne Boleyn, by Cromwell, and by the new archbishop whom events had required, Thomas Cranmer (1489–1556). Cranmer, serving as an ambassador in Germany, had just acquired a wife, and some protestant opinions, when he learned, no doubt to his horror, what his next job was to be. The revolution was even pushed forward by Henry himself, who became enthusiastic for a campaign to suppress the cults and centres of pilgrimage (such as Walsingham) and to demote the saints and destroy their images. And the monasteries were all too soft a target. Their destruction strengthened royal control of the Church and, so long as the money lasted, which was not long, more than doubled the revenues of the Crown. People were now to be told what to believe, by the king, and, if only for reasons of foreign diplomacy, official doctrine edged a little closer to Lutheranism. However, there were countervailing, conservative forces, including the other half of the king's religious brain which still clung strongly to the doctrine of the real presence in the Mass and other traditional things. Not long before the fall of Cromwell (as a heretic as well as a failed foreign secretary who had made a mess of Henry's fourth marriage, to Anne of Cleves), reactionary legislation was brought in to defend some of these things with stringent penalties, and Archbishop Cranmer was obliged to pack his wife and children off to Germany.

With the death of Henry VIII in 1547 and the accession of his nine-year-old son (the child of his third marriage, to Jane Seymour) as Edward VI, political alignments put the Reformation back on the road. Strangely enough, Henry, ever enigmatic when it came to religion, seems to have intended this, having done nothing to prevent his precious son from being brought up as a Protestant. The Reformation as negation now as never before touched ordinary people through the dissolution of chantries and guilds. Cranmer had an almost free hand. In official sermons, to be read out in all the churches, he preached the Lutheran scheme of salvation. Sinful man of necessity had to seek for 'another righteousness' which, 'embraced by faith', was 'taken, accepted, and allowed of God for our perfect and full justification'. Not that faith excluded the doing of good works: 'But it excludeth them, so that we may not do them to this intent, to be made good by doing of them.' That, however, was almost the extent of Cranmer's Lutheranism. In other respects he, and England with him, leant towards the emergent Reformed tradition and especially to the modified Zwinglian-ism of its eucharistic doctrine and practice. Leading reformers of this persuasion, including Martin Bucer, Peter Martyr Vermigli and, the most radical, the Polish nobleman Jan Laski (1499–1560), were made welcome at Lambeth. What had been the most national of reformations was internationalized.

England's religion was now fundamentally changed. Cranm-er's Book of Common Prayer rationalized the pattern of church services and turned everything into English. Clear articulation was emphasized, which obliged composers like Thomas Tallis to write a different kind of church music. Above all, the Mass was replaced by a service of commemorative Communion, or Lord's Supper, in which Cranmer emphasized the once-for-all efficacy of Christ's sacrifice of himself on the cross. In the first version of the Prayer Book (1549) there was a limited amount of structural change, intended to persuade those willing to be so persuaded that nothing much had changed. Cranmer himself was a conservative liturgist whose genius lay in the skilful adaptation of traditional prayers into beautiful English. However, they were not deceived in Devon and Cornwall, where there was armed resistance, which was put down by Spanish and German mercenaries. In 1552 Parliament enacted a second and less ambiguously protestant Prayer Book. Towards the end of the reign the Reformed doctrine of the Church of England was defined in the Forty-Two Articles, later revised as Thirty-Nine.

This was the high point of a roller-coaster of a Reformation. The printer's ink on the Prayer Book of 1552 was scarcely dry when Edward VI died, to be replaced, after the only successful Tudor rebellion (against the involuntary pretender, Lady Jane Grey), by his catholic half-sister Mary, who soon underlined the character of her regime by marriage to her cousin Philip of Spain. Historians in the protestant tradition have written of the Marian Reaction, as if the new turn of events was only negative and almost as if it was doomed from the start. The restoration of the Mass and return to the Roman obedience were certainly Counter-Reformation in the reactive sense. Historians better disposed towards Catholicism have written of a Marian Reformation, for the religion now reintroduced was more than a sterile return to all the old ways. If Mary had not died, childless, within six years of her accession, there is really no reason why Catholicism should not have stuck, rendering the Protestant Reformation a temporary aberration and itself more negative than otherwise, since while churches had been gutted and, in the case of the monasteries, demolished, hearts and minds had yet to be converted.

As things turned out, the Marian episode was significant as a paradox, almost as if its scenario was intended to prepare the way for the protestant triumph of Elizabeth's accession in 1558. Much of the future leadership of a protestant restoration had gone into exile in Germany and Switzerland, strengthening the bonds with Zürich, Geneva and other Reformed centres, while in England the persecution of heretics on an unprecedented scale had proved to be a counterproductive policy. Three hundred 'martyrs' burned at the stake may not seem very many to a world inured to genocide and holocaust. But it represented seven per cent of the total of all those executed for heresy throughout Europe in the course of the century. The victims ranged from Archbishop Cranmer and four other bishops to poor and ordinary people, including an illiterate Cardiff fisherman, many women, one of them blind, and several teenagers.

In Elizabeth's reign John Foxe made brilliant propaganda out of these atrocities in his regularly expanded *Acts and Monuments of the Church*, the largest book ever published in England and popularly known as the 'Book of Martyrs'. This was the most radical piece of historical revisionism ever undertaken, since Foxe placed the whole history of the Church on its head: so-called heresy was truth; 'catholic' truth was false (and cruel). The imaginative impact of Foxe was so great as to make it hard to know whether the burnings caused much revulsion at the time. However, Colchester in Essex, which was not a protestant town before the persecution, became one as a result of it; and in later years it served as a shrewd blow against a political opponent to accuse him of having been party to the persecution.

On Whitsunday 1559 England became once again an officially protestant nation. The Edwardian Prayer Book, now re-enacted with only a few changes, was again the only legal form of worship, with penalties for persistently breaking the law that included hefty fines and imprisonment for as much as a year. Even casual absence from church was in principle punishable with a fine of a shilling, two or three weeks' wages. But it took more than that to make a whole nation protestant. The minority of hot-gospellers, who called themselves 'the godly' and whom some denounced as 'Puritans', spoke darkly of 'cold statute protestants'. An inventive lexicography of stigmatizing abuse is evidence in itself of how deeply divided the English people had become. Catholics were called 'papists', presently distinguished as between 'popish recusants', from their outright and often costly refusal to attend protestant services, and the more compromising and compromised 'church papists'.

Conversion of the Elizabethans to a more than merely legal and formal Protestantism depended above all on the capacity of the clergy to preach and catechize the new doctrines; and preachers were at first in short supply, even wholly absent in some regions. It was not until the 1570s that things began to change, as the universities sent out into the parishes increasing numbers of protestant graduates, encouraged by the bishops and advanced by the political clout of some very powerful people, including Queen Elizabeth's favourite of favourites, Robert Dudley, earl of Leicester. If we are looking at London, the south-eastern counties, East Anglia and the east midlands, England was becoming a protestant country as the century neared its end. Religion of different kinds could still be found in pockets, but the largest pockets, almost becoming the coat itself, were exposed to and indoctrinated by a Protestantism that approximated to the religion of Reformed Europe. It was a different picture in large parts of the north, especially Lancashire, and here the process of Protestantization, never complete, happened in the first half of the seventeenth century. The influence of London, the centre of everything including not only government but the book trade, was so great that the export of the Reformation to the provinces has been called a 'London colonial enterprise'. If England in 1600 was not wholly Protestant, it was largely anti-Catholic, a nation that in the seventeenth century almost defined itself and its monarchy by its antipathy to 'popery'.

That this is less than the whole picture is due in very large measure to one person, Queen Elizabeth I. Elizabeth was celebrated as a protestant paragon, even as the head of Christ's Church on earth as the pope was head of the false Church. But much of this was window-dressing. No doubt Elizabeth was some kind of Protestant. Her origins, her claim to the throne, her foreign diplomacy, all made that a necessity, regardless of her personal opinions, which, while as opaque as those of any monarch, seem to have been protestant. But certainly not hot protestant: she was no Calvinist, and indeed her evident belief in some kind of real presence put her closer to Lutheranism. She habitually used old-fashioned catholic oaths such as 'By God's Body!' which curdled the blood of hot Protestants. She was attached to images that hot Protestants wanted to smash. But for her, it is likely that England's great cathedrals would have gone the same way as the monasteries, and with them the great tradition of English church music. Elizabeth seems to have preferred an old-fashioned celibate clergy. And she was no friend of preaching. Her second archbishop of Canterbury, who was sacked for refusing to countenance the suppression of a special kind of preaching (on the Zürich model) called 'prophesying', was horrified to hear her say that two or three preachers were sufficient for a whole county: 'Alas, Madam!'

The implications for policy were extensive. The religious settlement on which the Elizabethan Church was founded was deliberately moderated, especially in respect of what one bishop called 'the scenic apparatus' of religion. That set up a campaign among hot Protestants for a 'Further Reformation', which the queen used her bishops to suppress but which never went away, soon becoming still further radicalized with some Puritans demanding the abolition of both Prayer Book and episcopacy. Policy towards Catholics at home was more moderate than many Protestants wanted it to be, as Elizabeth did her best to blunt the edge of a war against terrorism that sent many Jesuits and other missionary priests and their supporters to the most hideous and undignified of deaths. Elizabeth spared the life of Mary, Queen of Scots, who was effectively her prisoner, for sixteen years after the Protestant political nation had first demanded her head on a charger. So far as foreign relations were concerned, Elizabeth refused to allow her policy to be dominated by anti-Catholic ideology rather than a more traditional and cautious realpolitik. On all these fronts she had the greater part of her government against her.

The Elizabethan compromise may have been politic but it created a rift between a conformist and defensive establishment and puritan nonconformity. Puritanism was much more than a quarrel with the Elizabethan settlement. It is hardly an exaggeration to say that it was the real English Reformation: an extensive programme of national renewal which aspired to reform popular culture, everything from maypoles, football, plays and pubs to speech and dress code, and above all the use of Sunday, now called the Sabbath – a set of values that applied the Old Testament to life much as some Muslim regimes apply shariah law, and, yes, it included the death penalty for adultery, although puritan ministers lacked the power of imams and ayatollahs to activate it. Godly Protestantism also had much to do with the growth in educational provision and the creation of a system of social welfare (the Elizabethan Poor Law), which were among the more notable achievements of the age. Puritanism consisted, at its heart, of something called 'practical divinity', a strenuous search for salvation according to Calvinist understandings.

The Irish Reformation is a perfect example of the 'London colonial enterprise', lacking many authentically indigenous features. That Ireland was a colonial enterprise in the more usual sense is more than half the reason for the failure of the Irish Reformation, as well as for the fusion of Catholicism and national(ist) sentiment in modern Ireland. Ironically it was Mary, the Catholic, who began the policy of colonial plantations in Ireland. These were not inevitable developments, however. In another part of the Gaelic world, the Western Isles of Scotland, the Reformation was a success, mostly because it expressed and propagated itself in the Gaelic language and through the traditional bardic culture, as youthful fiddlers and harp-players learned to sing the Psalms of David. Franciscan friars from Ireland found they were not welcome, while good presbyterian ministers from the south were scandalized by the long hair and scarcely decent garb of their no less godly island brethren. Wales could have taught the same lesson, although Wales was not Ireland and Tudor policy suffered from kidding itself that it was.

In Ireland the new faith was propagated from the English-speaking Dublin Pale, and it never learned to speak Irish. The English Reformation statutes, Henrician, Edwardian, Elizabethan, were rubber-stamped by the Irish Parliament (Henry VIII had made Ireland a kingdom, albeit a subordinate kingdom without a crown that English monarchs never visited), and the Irish monasteries and friaries (important centres of vibrant religious life in the fifteenth century) were dissolved in the areas under effective rather than nominal English control. The Prayer Book of 1549 was introduced in English and in Latin, not in Gaelic. There was no Gaelic New Testament until 1603. And there was little or no effective protestant evangelism. John Bale, one of the most dynamic of evangelical propagandists, who exploited the drama as well as the pulpit, was made an Irish bishop and should have been an effective missionary. But not in Ireland, where he was taken hostage by 'the wild Irish' and ransomed for a price. Bale put on the title page of his account of these adventures a quotation from the Psalms: 'God hath delivered me from the snare of the hunter / and from the noysome pestilence.' Most English writing on the subject of Ireland was in this vein, culminating in Edmund Spenser's truly colonialist book, *A view of the state of Ireland* (written by 1596 but not published until 1633).

All the running was made from the other side, by friars who were agents of the Counter-Reformation, trained in continental seminaries and now beginning to lay the foundations of that newly fashioned Catholicism that has been inseparable from our idea of Ireland. The lack of an Irish university was part of the problem. Too many preachers were failed English clergy on the run. When Trinity College, Dublin, was founded in 1592 it was almost too late. It was certainly too late, thirty years later, for William Bedell, its most enlightened provost and later the best of Irish bishops, to insist that the products of Trinity should be able to communicate in Gaelic. Bedell's fate was worse than Bale's. When northern Ireland exploded in rebellion in 1641, he led a column of refugees trying to make it to the coast but expired of typhus on the way.

Scotland was an altogether more complicated case. There was a moment in the Scottish Reformation when English military and political intervention saved it from collapse, and thereafter a state of amity existed. In the words of a Scottish contemporary, there was a degree of 'conformity with England', while Protestants who were dissatisfied with the level of reformation attained in England looked with envy at the Scottish model. But if the churches were mutually influential, there was never any question of an ecclesiastical union, which is not on anyone's agenda even in 2002.

The Scottish Reformation was home-grown, not made in England. In the mid-sixteenth century an 'auld alliance' with France, centuries old, became something more than that as Scotland bounced out of the embrace of Henry VIII, who wanted to annex the junior kingdom through a marriage between the infant Mary, Queen of Scots, and his son. Mary was first betrothed and soon married to the French dauphin, while her French mother, Mary of Guise, became regent, with French garrisons in Edinburgh Castle, Leith and other strongholds. The Scottish protestant movement was almost as old as the Reformation itself, but only now did it begin to organize itself as an alternative Church, which made common cause with a rebellious association of the nobility who called themselves 'Lords of the Congregation'.

This was reformation by means of revolution, a pattern repeated more than once in the century to come. This alarmed some English observers. John Knox (c.1514–72), self-appointed prophet to the revolution, was *persona non grata* in England in consequence of his political views. When Mary Stuart returned to Scotland, a French widow, he appointed her Jezebel to his Elijah, reducing her to tears in his sermons and audiences (where she did all the listening). But Knox was an Anglicized Scot, who told Elizabeth's minister, William Cecil, that he had always desired 'a perpetual concord betwixt these two realms'. Cecil wanted that too, and although he disliked what he called 'Knox's audacity' he was content to use him in a grand and adventurous design that saved the bacon of the Lords of the Congregation, got the French out of Scotland, and achieved an alliance between London and Edinburgh. Scotland was a theatre of international politics that required constant diplomatic attention. However, it was now to be hoped that unity in the fundamentals of religion would be a better defence of England's northern frontier than the forts that the English government had built and garrisoned, at punitive cost, in the 1540s, and that it would in due course ease a closer unity of the two kingdoms – which happened in 1603 when Mary Stuart's son, James VI, became James I of England.

In so far as ecclesiastical relations were strained, and strained to the extent of war in the reign of James's son, Charles I, this was less the fault of Knox than of the kind of church–state relations that the Scottish Reformation created and of the hard men who came after Knox. In Scotland there was no royal supremacy, and while the Crown had ways and means of intervening and managing, ultimate authority in the affairs of the Kirk in principle belonged to a General Assembly, which was bound by a kind of ecclesiastical constitution, the Book of Discipline. The old Church had never been dismantled and its bishops, who still existed, were looked upon with suspicion as cat's-paws employed to secure greater royal control of the Kirk's affairs and resources. When Andrew Melville (1545–1622) returned to Scotland from Theodore Beza's Geneva, he and others took advantage of the opportunity that these still fluid arrangements provided, and of the instability of Scottish politics, to reorganize the Kirk along presbyterian lines with local kirk sessions (of pastors, elders and deacons), regional presbyteries, and a national General Assembly under a revised Book of Discipline. This was as much anti-monarchical as it was anti-prelatical. Melville told James VI on one occasion that there were two kingdoms in Scotland, not one, and that in the kingdom of Christ he was 'naught but a silly vassal'. Small wonder that, as James I, the king famously pronounced, 'no bishop, no king'. In practice, though, the Kirk was an unstable amalgam of episcopal and presbyterian elements. Still to come were the Bishops' Wars, which in turn precipitated the English Civil War.

Looking back on these exceptional cases, what happened to 'these islands', in terms of religion, in the sixteenth century proves to have been responsible to a considerable extent for what they have been almost ever since. These were at once cataclysmic and creative events of the greatest historical magnitude, a series of long-lasting cultural revolutions. In England they left behind a mongrel Anglicanism that deluded itself that nothing much had really changed, and which possesses to this day the high ground of national life, while confronting a Protestant Nonconformity and a resurgent Catholicism strong enough to defy its claim to be a truly national Church. In Scotland, the mostly Presbyterian Kirk, especially through the operations of its kirk sessions, remodelled the nation in ways that to a modern observer may seem simultaneously repressive and enlightened. (That Scotland is better at educating its children than England is one long-term consequence of that remodelling.) In Ireland the Reformation was almost wholly counterproductive but also creative, not so much because it perpetuated the old Ireland as because the provocation of a colonial enterprise forged a new one.

9 Politics

Cuius regio, eius religio. The pithy phrase was coined in the early seventeenth century to convey the gist of the Religious Peace of Augsburg, signed on 25 September 1555, which recognized the existence in the Holy Roman Empire of two confessional parties, Catholics and Lutherans (Zwinglians, Calvinists and Anabaptists were excluded from its terms). Augsburg was intended as no more than a stopgap, but it remained in force until the Empire itself was wound up in Napoleonic times. The meaning of the formula is that rulers (electors, princes, dukes and counts) have the right to determine the religion of their subjects, who, if they are unhappy with the decision made over their heads, may sell their property and emigrate.

This was far from religious toleration, although the imperial cities were free to pursue the values of live and let live by allowing both confessions, where they were both present, to coexist in the practice of their religion. There was a certain amount of nodding and winking that condoned a plurality of confessions, not just the biconfessionalism of Augsburg. Lutheran Nuremberg opened its gates to Calvinist merchants and artisans from the Netherlands, and even offered tax breaks to attract them.

Such exceptions aside, the *cuius regio, eius religio* principle drew the confessional map of sixteenth-century Europe. And since most of Europe's monarchs and other major territorial rulers saw no reason to change their religion to any of the Protestant confessions on offer, it determined that the greater part of the Continent remained Catholic: the Iberian monarchies; Italy; France (when the protestant Henry IV came to the throne he soon converted – Paris was worth a mass); most German principalities, including Bavaria (where the Wittelsbachs ruled from 1180 to 1918); Habsburg Austria; those parts of the Netherlands that remained under Spanish rule. Among the monarchies, only Scandinavia would adopt Lutheranism. This was a pure form of *cuius regio, eius religio*, since in Denmark/Norway under Frederick I (1523–33) and Sweden/Finland, newly independent from Denmark under Gustavus Vasa (1523–60), there was no popular pressure for reform and subsequently virtually no dissent. No more than Henry VIII were Frederick and Gustavus enthusiastic devotees of a new religion called Protestantism, although their successors, like Henry's, were. Lutheran Scandinavia was peripheral to the sixteenth century, but it acquired geopolitical importance in the Thirty Years' War of the seventeenth when there was a Swedish moment, the moment of Gustavus Adolphus, that saved the bloody but unbowed cause of pan-European Protestantism.

England was a rogue card, but under the Tudors a perfect example of an entirely pragmatic *cuius regio, eius religio*: bound to follow the twists and turns of Henry VIII's idiosyncratic religious mind, then Protestant under Edward VI, Catholic under Mary, Protestant again under Elizabeth. Since the difference of religion meant that there were no suitable husbands to be found among the crowned heads and archdukes of Europe, Elizabeth remained single and heirless. Consequently, in the event of her death, her subjects might well have found themselves subjects of another Mary who would have made them Catholics all over again (if they had let her). That possibility lasted for a quarter of a century, with a hardly less anxious sequel to Mary Stuart's execution in 1587, which ended only with the unexpectedly smooth succession of her son, James VI and I, in 1603. James was a Protestant, but he was the only member of his family in seven generations whose Protestantism could be relied upon. The history of the Stuarts in the seventeenth century suggests that they found in Catholicism, or something very like it, the most appropriate ideological foundation and symbolic dressing for the kind of monarchy they were interested in promoting: a fatal attraction, as things worked out. The execution of Charles I in 1649 and the deposition of James II in 1688 prove that there were limits to the principle of *cuius regio, eius religio*.

Almost everywhere there was a mismatch between governments of one religious persuasion and subjects of another. Minds were not yet elastic enough to contain the idea of a tolerated state of religious pluralism. In Elizabethan England a politician made a speech in which he said that if religion were to cease to be uniform and to become 'milliform' it would finish up 'nulliform'. So under Mary Protestants had to choose between death by burning, exile and, the most popular choice, keeping their heads down. Those who outwardly conformed, in France as well as England, Calvin disparaged as 'Nicodemites', followers of that Nicodemus who came to Jesus by night (John 3:2). Catholics under Elizabeth faced similar choices in consequence of increasingly draconian laws, including death by disembowelment, exile, or the closet existence of church papists. *Cuius regio, eius religio* made many martyrs from all faiths, destroyed families and broke consciences, a heavy price to pay for the stability of the state. Not that it made for a stable state either. Dissent was beyond the capacity of the sixteenth-century state to eliminate entirely, and the threat it was thought to pose was often a self-fulfilling prophecy. In some cases, minority religion offered the possibility of resistance and even an alternative, which was to turn the principle upside down: *cuius religio, eius regio*.

It is perhaps surprising that relatively few sixteenth-century rulers found Protestantism attractive. Martin Luther made a strong pitch for their support in his *Open Letter to the Christian Nobility of the German Nation*. As Henry VIII discovered in England and Gustavus Vasa in Sweden, there were obvious advantages to invading ecclesiastical jurisdiction and appropriating ecclesiastical property. When William Tyndale taught in his *The Obedience of a Christian Man* (1528) that the monarch was not to be resisted but was 'in this world without law and may at his lust do right or wrong and shall give accounts but to God only', Henry is supposed to have said, 'This is a book for me and all kings to read.'

Luther's politics were admittedly double-edged, conditioned by what scholarship knows as his *Zwei-Reiche-Lehre*, or Two Kingdoms Doctrine. He separated the spiritual government of God and his word, *das geistliche Regiment*, from temporal government, *das weltliche Regiment* or even *Teufels Reich*, the Devil's rule. If the world were fully Christian, there would be no need of government, but since it was not, Christians must be prepared to serve in government, even, as he once wrote, to supply a shortage of hangmen. 'It is not man but God who hangs and breaks on the wheel and beheads and strangles.'

Only Luther could have written a book with the title *Whether Soldiers, Too, Can Be Saved* (1527). They could, but temporal rulers were warned not to lay their hands on the sacred ark, especially in Luther's most important writing on the subject, *Secular Authority: To What Extent It Should Be Obeyed* (1523) – not all the way and not in all things. Luther explained that in this book he had deliberately changed the tactics of the *Open Letter* because the nobility were taking too much upon themselves. 'God Almighty has made our rulers mad. They actually think they have the power to do and command their subjects to do whatever they please.' It is thought that this was aimed at Duke George 'the Bearded' of Saxony, the other Saxon prince, who resisted reform in his own territory and hemmed it in in Luther's own Electoral Saxony. Later, Henry of England became the target and Luther said some very shocking things in print about that anointed monarch.

So it is clear that even with Luther Protestantism was not merely an ideological fig-leaf for the excesses of tyranny. In the Second World War the leading Lutheran scholar in England published a book titled *Luther, Hitler's Cause or Cure?* (He thought, cure.) On the other hand, the Two Kingdoms Doctrine could be understood to rule out the kind of intervention of religious men and motives in temporal matters that became a hallmark of Calvinism. In August 1914, the top-ranking Lutheran divines of Germany explained that the Great War being undertaken could only be defensive, Lutheranism being Lutheranism. In their perception, the British Empire, which justified itself as a mission to humankind, was a Calvinist thing and confused the two kingdoms. There could never be a Lutheran *jihad*.

Textbooks used to teach that it was simple self-interest that attracted rulers to Protestantism. Similarly, Lutheran preachers and publicists found it politic to underwrite the powers that be, especially after the bad scare of the Peasants' War. Luther would not perhaps have written *Of Secular Authority* after 1525. But in so far as the decisions involved were pragmatic, it is not clear that the calculus always pointed to the protestant option. Francis I of France did not need to do a Henry VIII in order to enjoy religious as well as temporal ascendancy in France, where popes rarely got their toe in the door and that most Catholic king Louis XIV was all that those nominally protestant Stuarts would like to have been. The Bavarian Wittelsbachs did not need to turn Protestant in order to stand up to their ancient enemies, the Habsburgs.

Rulers who were faced with a religious choice, even Henry VIII, actually had minds and consciences. It is also relevant that they were advised by chancellors and secretaries of state who were humanists and often sympathetic to reform. In the case of the most enthusiastically protestant of the German princes, Philip, the landgrave of Hesse, it is proper to speak of a conversion. Admittedly this was advantageous. Although the lesser nobility of Hesse insisted on having a say in the employment of ex-ecclesiastical revenues, some of which (fifty-nine per cent) went to fund four hospitals and the new University of Marburg, the rest was devoted to the needs of the prince and the state. All this carried a risk, however, and had a price. After Charles V defeated the Protestant princes in the Schmalkaldic War, Philip was to spend five years in prison.

Whatever the motives and what historians, to save themselves a lot of trouble, call 'factors', the politico-religious map of Germany looked like this thirty years after Luther first appeared above the horizon. Electoral Saxony remained staunchly Evangelical under the successors of Frederick the Wise, the leading Protestant power in the Empire. With the added muscle of Philip of Hesse, Electoral Saxony was the core of the defensive military federation formed in 1530 and known as the Schmalkald League, a disturbing development that was prompted by what was almost certainly a mischievous leak to the effect that the Catholic princes were in secret league against Electoral Saxony and Hesse. That followed the Diet of Speyer

(1529) when an attempt to resuscitate the 1521 edict outlawing Lutheranism provoked the protestation of six Lutheran princes and fourteen cities, giving us the convenient nickname Protestant. In the following year the Lutheran estates of the Empire presented another diet with the Confession of Augsburg, a conciliatory document drafted by Philipp Melanchthon and too mealy-mouthed for the banned Luther, who was able to approach no closer to Augsburg and the imperial presence than the castle of Coburg. The Swiss and the south German cities tabled their own confessions of faith. Luther need not have worried, however. Although the Confession of Augsburg was a definitive statement of Lutheranism in the long term, in the short term it was not the basis for a religious settlement and there was stalemate. What protected the Evangelical cause were such 'factors' as the reluctance of the Catholic princes to see any further extension of Habsburg power and the prime need to resist the advance of the Turks.

The other Saxony, Albertine Saxony, joined the cause in 1539. In 1525 Luther had persuaded Albert of Hohenzollern, grand master of the Teutonic Knights and ruler of Prussia, to secularize his office and accept it as a fief from the Polish crown (a lot of European history in the making). Another prince of the Hohenzollern family, the Margrave Casimir of Ansbach-Bamberg (whose territory adjoined Nuremberg), also adopted Lutheranism. Brunswick, lying to the south of Bremen and Hamburg, and the counts of Mansfeld went the same way. By now, especially with the Hanseatic cities of the Baltic region added in, Germany was split by a north–south divide: the north Lutheran; the south, except for some of the imperial cities, Catholic. But in the mid 1530s some dramatic politics in the south-western duchy of Württemberg altered the map. Duke Ulrich (1487–1550) had been expelled by the forces of the coalition of cities and territories known as the Swabian League and his duchy sold to the Habsburgs. In 1534 he was restored by Philip of Hesse, with the help of some French money. Ulrich had become a Zwinglian and proceeded to reform his duchy, helping himself in the process to a great deal of church property. Württemberg became a protestant salient in the south, pulled in different directions by Lutheranism and Zwinglianism. It is a part of Germany that has remained protestant to this day.

The most remarkable single fact about the German Reformation is its success in the towns, of which there were around three thousand, and especially in the imperial cities (*Reichstadte*), which were estates of the Empire in their own right and subject only to the emperor. Of sixty-five imperial cities, more than fifty officially accepted the Reformation at some point in the sixteenth century and only a handful remained unaffected. We must not be carried away, however. Most of what is known concerns the larger cities with populations of between ten and twenty thousand, and there were only two dozen of those. Most towns contained less than two thousand people. Moreover, townspeople represented no more than five per cent of the German population, so the famed urban reformation affected no more than half a per cent of the nation. Nevertheless, the reception of the Gospel in such major cities as Nuremberg, Strassburg, Augsburg and Regensburg invites explanation.

The beneficiaries of religious change, as well as the agents who took the necessary decisions, were the city councils, so that the Reformation in the towns can be seen as not so much the turning of a new page in their history as the last chapter in a medieval story that for some time had been eroding ecclesiastical power to the advantage of the civil magistracy. Long before the Reformation, bishops were actually excluded from, for example, Strassburg, and only on strict conditions was the archbishop of Cologne allowed to enter the city, the German Rome. The magistracy had long considered poor relief and the regulation of sexual and marital matters to be its business. Now it was magistrates and town councils who took over monasteries and expelled monks and priests, abolished the Mass and religious processions, appointed preachers and even told them what to say. There were new opportunities for city leaders of stature, typified by the commanding figure of Jacob Sturm (1489–1553), *Stettmeister* of Strassburg and architect of the Schmalkald League, a greater statesman than any of the crowned heads of Europe of the time.

But Protestantism was not imposed on an unwilling populace. Most studies suggest that the pressure for reform came from below, or from the urban commune as a whole, with the ultimate agency often to be found in the critical, prophetic voice of the pulpit: Bucer and his colleagues in Strassburg; Oecolampadius in Basle; Archbishop Cranmer's uncle-in-law, Osiander, in Nuremberg; and let us not forget the fire-eating Müntzer in Allstedt and Mühlhausen. Religious change arose from a dialectic between pressure groups and the authorities, governments and the governed, with the magistracy, whose first duty was to keep order, often forced to acknowledge that the all-important peace and unity of the city were to be sought by embracing reform rather than attempting to suppress it.

Some historians have viewed the urban commune through distinctly rosy spectacles, with the overture to Wagner's *Meistersinger von Nürnberg* providing the background music to an idealized *Gemeindereformation*. Their more hard-headed colleagues have reminded us that the German city was a highly fractionalized society, riddled with conflict, a place where women, apprentices, servants and labourers, all of whom must have had opinions, had no say. The image of a unified and idealized commune was so much spin-doctoring. Cities where those in charge were responsive to the demands of the citizenry at large, and where the political contexts in which they operated allowed them to be responsive, were perhaps exceptional rather than typical. In the words of one leading historian, the Reformation in the cities was not a wonder-working social superglue.

In July 1546, Charles V at last found a window of opportunity to move militarily against the Protestant forces of the League of Schmalkald, a window created by his having come to terms with the Turks and the French and secured a large mercenary force paid for by Pope Paul III. The decisive events in a winter war of nine months were the defection from the Protestant cause of Duke Moritz of Albertine Saxony, who had left the League in 1542 convinced that the issue was not religion but the integrity of the German Reich, and the decisive defeat of the Elector John Frederick of Ernestine Saxony at the bloody rout of Mühlberg on 24 April 1547. Both John Frederick and Philip of Hesse were stripped of lands and titles.

However, this was a pyrrhic victory. Charles had the physical but not the moral means to impose his own religious settlement on the protestant estates of the Empire (and only Protestants, not Catholics, were selected for this treatment) in a so-called Interim, since the official line was still that the General Council would solve all problems. This included the middle-way doctrine of double justification and conceded clerical marriage and the cup for the laity, but was otherwise a conservative affirmation of Catholicism. The Interim succeeded in dividing and confusing all parties. Melanchthon was never forgiven by uncompromising Lutherans (the so-called Gnesio-Lutherans, from the Greek *gnesios*, born in wedlock, hence legitimate) for having made concessions to the Interim, nor for a letter in which he confessed: 'At times earlier in life I followed Luther too slavishly.' (Luther had died four months before the war.) More to the point, Moritz of Saxony realized that the Interim was no use, made common cause with France, and headed a new alignment of princes that outfaced the emperor (the Princes' Revolt). This led to the Religious Peace of Augsburg and the withdrawal of Charles V from politics. Moritz died in the midst of these events but Albertine Saxony remained protestant until 1679.

With the emperor's Spanish troops at large in Germany, the Reformation had been crushed in some cities, including Constance, while others, among them Strassburg and Nuremberg (which had remained neutral in the war), were forced to accept the Interim over the metaphorical dead bodies of their preachers. Osiander of Nuremberg found a new life for himself in (east) Prussia and Bucer of Strassburg in Cambridge, where the appalling climate soon finished him off.

It was in the course of these events that one of Germany's greatest and most historic cities, Magdeburg, played a role that, in retrospect, has been seen as significant in the history of political rights. Magdeburg became a stronghold of hardline Lutheran resistance to the Interim, led by Luther's old colleague and Staupitz's nephew, Nikolaus von Amsdorf (1483–1565), who had become one of the first Lutheran bishops, and the young Croatian layman Matthias Flacius Illyricus (1520–75), later organizer of the massive protestant church history known as the *Magdeburg Centuries*. Out of Magdeburg, somewhat cynically besieged by Duke Moritz as an imperial commander (the whole thing was eventually wound up on mutually advantageous terms), came a *Bekenntnis* (confession), justifying the military resistance of 'lesser magistrates' to the imperial power as not so much a right as a duty. With a certain amount of poetic licence it has been said that this was the last time that the voice of the people was heard in Germany before the eighteenth century. The Magdeburg *Bekenntnis* proved to be a document of European importance. Outside Germany it was a seed that bore fruit among British exiles in Geneva, and later among French and Dutch revolutionary Calvinists and in Scotland.

In 1558 there were Catholic regimes in both England and Scotland, and in England Protestants had suffered four years of fire and faggot at the hands of the woman the nineteenth century would call Bloody Mary. The Anglicized Scot John Knox was not to know that Mary was about to be succeeded by her protestant sister, who would put out the fires and welcome the protestant exiles back from Germany and Switzerland. In 1558 he had published, at Geneva, *The First blast of the trumpet against the monstrous regiment of women*. 'Monstrous regiment' meant unnatural rule, and Knox had found in divine and natural law reasons why Mary Tudor's government – and so, it followed, Elizabeth's too – was illegitimate, unless God made an exception and dispensed with the law. Knox was not welcome. In the same year, Knox's closest friend, the English exile Christopher Goodman (1520?–1603) published, also in Geneva, *How superior powers oght to be obeyd of their subjects*, which explained in the remainder of a long title how when they become tyrants they ought to be disobeyed. Two years earlier John Ponet (1514?–56), a bishop under Edward VI, had published at Strassburg, anonymously, *A shorte treatise of politike power, and of the true obedience which subjectes owe to kynges and other civile governours*. Once again, 'true obedience' proved in some circumstances to be disobedience.

The cat of resistance theory was out of the bag, the start of the modern politics we call ideological.

Both Ponet and Goodman were truly radical in that they did not restrict the duty to oppose tyranny to those 'inferior magistrates' who had public office and responsibility. All members of the community, 'the common people also', were entitled not only to resist and restrain but to assassinate evil governors. For if magistrates and other officers failed in their duty the people were 'as it were without officers'. This was a licence to kill for the Lee Harvey Oswalds of this world. Ponet did not mention Mary Tudor by name and directed his rhetorical artillery against her murderous bishops. For Goodman, however, it was the queen herself, an 'open idolatress', who fully deserved death.

Knox followed up his *First blast* with a succession of pamphlets directed at the situation in Scotland, in which he was soon actively involved as the prophetic voice of revolution. The *Second blast of the trumpet* was never completed, but we know that if Knox had published it it would have expounded a fully rounded politics of resistance. Rulers, including kings, hold their power not by inheritance but by election and are accountable to those who have elected them. An idolater elected to such an office can and should be deposed. That is what happened when in 1567 Mary, Queen of Scots, was deposed in favour of her infant son and forced out of Scotland into her English captivity, an event that deeply shocked Catholic Europe, but not Protestant England, where she was described in the House of Commons as no longer a queen but 'the monstrous and huge dragon and mass of the earth'. One MP said: 'My advice is to cut off her head and make no more ado about her,' which echoed words used about the wicked

Queen Jezebel in the Old Testament. And that was what eventually happened, but not without some ado.

The most learned Scottish humanist of his generation, George Buchanan (1506–82), tutor to James VI, built such events into a fully developed political theory in his *De jure regni apud Scotos* and a *History of Scotland*, both published between 1579 and 1582. Deploying arguments derived from classical republicanism, Buchanan argued that kings were neither more nor less than public officers chosen to perform defined functions. If they failed to deliver, the people who had elected them had the right to dismiss them. Buchanan claimed the authority of two thousand years of Scottish history, and cited the precedents of a dozen kings who in the course of that partly fictitious history had been deposed. These lessons were counterproductive in the case of Buchanan's star pupil, who turned them upside down: kings rule by divine right.

John Calvin, who had said the same, was still alive and at the height of his powers and influence when the Geneva publisher Jean Crespin printed those inflammatory tracts by Knox and Goodman. Calvin did not approve. To the end of his days, he never sanctioned resistance to legal rulers. That included evil rulers, 'be their characters what they may'. Tyrants, too, were God's instruments. The closest Calvin came to allowing resistance was in the last edition of the *Institutes*, where he acknowledged that the constitutions of some states provided for 'popular magistrates' 'to curb the tyranny of kings': the ephors of Sparta, for example, or the tribunes of Rome, or 'perhaps' parliaments in modern kingdoms. But it was an idle occupation for private men to discuss what form of government they would choose to live under, although Calvin admitted that if he were to indulge in this piece of idleness he would prefer aristocracy to monarchy. Ever the cautious jurist, he would have allowed the military operations of the French 'Huguenots' (as French Protestants were nicknamed) if they had been commanded by the first prince of the blood. Unfortunately that illustrious personage Anthony of Bourbon, father of the future Henry IV, was a very unsatisfactory Protestant, a broken reed.

In the first three Wars of Religion, the Huguenots were able to hide behind the polite fiction that their quarrel was not with the king but with his evil advisers, principally the house of Guise. As long as the queen mother, Catherine de Medicis, held the ring that made sense. But the Massacre of St Bartholomew in August 1572, in which Catherine was fully complicit, was another 11 September moment in European history. Perhaps ten thousand people died in Paris and a dozen other cities. The massacre was seen as a Machiavellian plot, typical of Catherine's native Italy. A Huguenot who had escaped to Geneva, Innocent Gentillet, wrote a book called *Anti-Machiavel* which fixed for all time the image of Machiavelli as 'old Nick', Satan personified, a character best known in the shape of Shakespeare's Richard III and from Christopher Marlowe's *The Jew of Malta* where the Prologue is spoken by the character of Machiavel: 'I count religion but a childish toy / And hold there is no sin but ignorance.'

Large areas of southern France now became a federation of self-governing republics, a state within the state. Catholics responded by forming their own League, and when it became apparent that the heir to Henry III, the last of a family of brothers, would be the Protestant Henry of Bourbon, king of Navarre, the Catholic League became a revolutionary force organized to prevent his succession. Paris itself became a self-governing commune, its streets ruled by a committee representing its sixteen districts (*les seize*). In May 1588 there was a night of the barricades when the League seized control of the capital. Now it was a Catholic assassin, a Capuchin friar, who followed the advice of Christopher Goodman and stuck his dagger into the king's abdomen. It was revenge for the death of the Guise brothers, the duke and the cardinal, which Henry had ordered.

St Bartholomew had been followed by the unveiling of a French doctrine of resistance. Théodore de Bèze wrote *Du droit des magistrats* (1573), in which he went beyond Calvin in sanctioning resistance by inferior magistrates. But the most notable of these manifestos was the *Vindiciae contra tyrannos* (1579), probably the work of a young Huguenot nobleman, Philippe Du Plessis-Mornay, although the grey eminence behind the book may have been the diplomat Hubert Languet, friend and mentor to the Englishman Sir Philip Sidney. The *Vindiciae* argued that both king and subjects are in a contractual relationship with God. If the king fails in his duty, the inferior magistrates and even 'the least of the people' must honour their contract by removing him. However, since most 'people' in France, and especially in Paris, were still Catholics there was little incentive to develop Goodman's theory of popular resistance.

In the Netherlands, a constitutionally justified resistance to the onslaught on traditional privileges by the ruler, Philip II of Spain, was initially headed by leading 'inferior magistrates', including William of Orange, whose princely title in the south of France made his lifelong struggle against the Spanish tyrant more legitimate than it might otherwise have been. The Dutch Revolt was soon hijacked by Calvinist revolutionaries with the aid of an organization based on tightly disciplined religious communities, many led by preachers trained in Geneva. The rebels, nicknamed Beggars, took to the sea and gained a bridgehead in the northern province of Holland. From there they took over the government in town after town. In most cases the mere threat of force was enough to persuade the magistrates to open their gates to the Beggars who, once inside, imposed a drastic, iconoclastic reformation. The parallel with the twentieth-century Bolsheviks is striking, for in no proper sense was this revolution popular; in Alkmaar in 1576, for example, the Calvinist congregation numbered 160 in a town of six thousand inhabitants. In the great cities of Brabant and Flanders to the south power was seized from within by men of the artisan class, a long tradition in a place like Ghent. Once again the activists were a small minority of the population.

However, if you were to ask any well-informed Englishman towards the end of the sixteenth century who were the assassins and regicidal enemies of monarchy, he would have answered 'the papists', and with some justice. It was Jesuit theologians Cardinal Robert Bellarmine (1542–1621), Francisco de Suarez (1548–1617) and the Englishman Robert Parsons who developed a theology and casuistry of tyrannicide and deposition that was a mirror image of Calvinist politics, if differently rooted in scholastic philosophy, with the pope rather than Almighty God as the validator. According to Suarez, the pontiff was empowered 'to reprove even the greatest kings as if they were his subjects'. But this was not the opinion of all, or even most, Catholics.

Soon, in 1605, your Englishman, well informed or not, would have told you that it was the papists, Guy Fawkes and his gang, who had plotted to blow up the king and the entire political nation in the Houses of Parliament. That was an 11 September that never happened. If it had, someone would surely have declared a war against terrorism. Nevertheless, 'guys' are still burned on bonfires throughout England on 5 November, and in Lewes in Sussex they even burn an effigy of the pope.

10 *People*

The sixteenth century, for all its deference and hierarchy, sometimes invoked that convenient if elusive fiction 'the people'. Archbishop Cranmer insisted that his new form of church service, the Book of Common Prayer, should be 'understanded of the people'. The English martyrologist John Foxe filled his 'Book of Martyrs' with a cast of thousands, 'the godly multitude and congregation'. Frustrated by his failure to advance 'Further Reformation' by legitimate means, a puritan activist said that 'the people' must bring it to pass. But that was a compromising, even incriminating remark. John Knox's version of reformation in Scotland was a fearful precedent because he had made 'the people orderers of things'. 'The people' were feared.

When they were not feared they were patronized. It was assumed that they had ears, itching ears, but no brains. They would believe anything, think of nothing. It was certainly true that the vast majority of people in the sixteenth century, and all but a tiny minority of women, were illiterate, unable to read for themselves even pamphlets that were ostensibly aimed at their level. But that did not mean that people were without ideas and religious beliefs or were cut off from what was going on around them. Often the people themselves were doing it. The Reformation was also a popular movement.

It is easy to say that but, having said it, we need to ask ourselves what we mean by 'movement' (and, for that matter, by 'popular'). To use the word 'movement' promiscuously will deprive it of meaning. A movement was also a moment, like Wittenberg in 1521 or many of the events feeding into the Peasants' War. A movement involves numbers of people, a collectivity, whether of students or townspeople or peasants: something like what happened in Paris in 1968. The action must also be of a collective nature and expressive of some kind of common consciousness. It will consist of actions rather than arguments, although the actions may express a language of their own, a non-verbalized argument. The movement may be stimulated by words, in the form of a rousing sermon, and may find a voice in the words of psalms and hymns sung as protest songs. The purpose of such a movement will be to change the existing order of things, in this case traditional religious practice, although another kind of movement was aimed at the unpopular economic practices of men of property, such as enclosing common land or artificially forcing up the price of bread, resulting in enclosure riots or bread riots. Action of this kind was undertaken on a massive scale in 1525. The aim is rapid, even instant change: what we (but not the sixteenth century) call revolution, although the intentions of many early modern movements were conservative and counter-revolutionary, the desired change being a return to the way things had been and ought to be. The methods are those of direct action, outside established norms and procedures and against those who are supposed to be in control, who typically lose control at the moment of such a movement.

Something historians of such movements have to accept, even if they cannot altogether explain it, is how people knew what to do, how the libretto for such an opera was so thoroughly internalized. In many parts of Europe irregular social behaviour, a wife beating her husband or a notorious case of adultery, provoked a 'charivari' or (in English) 'rough riding', a carnivalesque ritual involving pots and pans, a set of horns with which to mock the unfortunate cuckold, a good supply of excrement, and a rich repertoire of insulting gestures, all supposedly expressing the disapproval of the community. In England the rarer abuses of buggery and bestiality were an occasion for a 'groaning'. Now how did people know what to do in a groaning?

By now it should be clear that to understand the Reformation as some sort of popular movement will require more than finding out how ideas, the theology of Martin Luther, for example, percolated down to passively receptive audiences. We return to a question briefly posed at the end of an earlier chapter. We may think that we know what Luther and other reformers were saying. But what were they *heard* to be saying? When the peasants understood Luther to be teaching a form of liberation theology, a social gospel, were they wrong? We are told that when Africans were told by missionaries about salvation through the blood of Jesus what they heard and understood was a message about physical healing. Were they mistaken? Even this, however, is to assume that the Reformation was simply a top-down process with the roles of communicator and receptor clearly differentiated. We need to go beyond an understanding of how ideas have been disseminated and received, and acknowledge the active agency of uneducated and, in the language of the time, 'simple' people.

There were four ways in which the people of the sixteenth century learned and shared new things: acted-out ritual, the spoken word, the written word (whether handwritten or printed), and pictures. In practice, these forms of communication were interactive. The sermon was probably the most powerful means of top-down oral communication, although even the sermon could lead to a two-way traffic in ideas, the hearers answering back, which often happened in Germany in the 1520s. There were also organized pulpit debates, disputations between rival preachers, with the hearers made the umpires. When the most popular preacher of the Reformation in England, Hugh Latimer, engaged in Bristol with a friar called William Hubardin, the debate ended when the pulpit collapsed under Hubardin's strenuous efforts, injuring his leg and causing his death. The churchwardens said that their pulpit was built for preaching, not for dancing. Plays were another form of oral propaganda, the vice figures of the traditional drama now dressed up as monks and priests. In England John Bale, who wrote plays for Thomas Cromwell, discovered that if an actor wearing a bishop's mitre were to bend down in front of the audience the mitre could be transformed into the jaws of a wolf. There was street theatre, too, and carnival, an acted-out inversion of an unpopular reality.

Sermons, like modern political speeches, were often reduced in the memories of those exposed to them to a single memorable and even shocking statement. Perhaps the preachers knew that. Successful preachers expressed themselves in the idiom of ordinary life, even what in England were called 'old saws'. So things uttered from the pulpit became part of that collection of proverbs that people carried about in their heads. Someone hearing a heretical sermon in Henry VIII's England would not forget that to pray to saints was but to worship 'stocks and stones and dead men's bones'. If he knew that already, so much the better to hear it confirmed from the mouth of a learned man.

Sermons could also be taken down in shorthand, published as books, and read. Latimer's sermons were printed in black letter, the typeface with which the unlearned were most familiar, making a populist pitch with their very appearance. However, religious books of even the simplest kind were closed books to most people, especially in Luther's Saxony where there were very few schools, and none in the countryside. Luther was horrified to discover, during the first church visitation of Saxony, how profoundly ignorant most people were of the most basic elements of religion. Nevertheless, people in the sixteenth century read aloud (most, it seems, lacked the capacity to read silently) so that any book, from Luther's or Tyndale's Bible to a scruffy little pamphlet, would have a potential audience of many non-readers. This might happen in church. When Henry VIII ordered the Bible to be set up in churches, groups gathered around it and listened. In St Paul's Cathedral a man gained notoriety for reading in such a loud voice that he drowned out the choir singing Mass. But readings and consequent discussions were just as likely to take place in the pub. The English reformer Thomas Wisdom was told off by his bishop for encouraging the sacred text to be manhandled by people who were drunk. Wisdom replied that if people took the Bible down to the pub on a Sunday evening they would not get drunk. Bishop Bonner's concern was justified, however, and there was soon need for legislation to curb the 'reviling' of the Mass in places where people gathered to drink. In Germany the spinning bee, a universal social institution among women given to gossip, was often an occasion for gossiping the Gospel.

In the west of England, heretics were called 'two-penny book men'. The most characteristic vehicle for Reformation ideas was the pamphlet, in German *Flugschrift*, comprising thirty-two pages of print, and sold for the equivalent of a day's wages. Before the pamphlets there were pictures and a habit of learning by looking rather than absorbing words. Preceding the invention of the printed book, woodcuts were the first item of mass communication. Three or four thousand copies of a cut could be made before the block wore out, and it has been estimated that they were sold in their tens of thousands, often to commemorate a religious experience, like the metal tokens bought by pilgrims – the picture postcards of the sixteenth century. Soon woodcuts of Martin Luther were given the same treatment, and rumours flew that in a house fire in this or that place the only thing to survive had been a piece of paper bearing Luther's image: 'incombustible' Luther.

With literacy on the increase the Reformation itself ensured that the pamphlet, sometimes illustrated but often not, would win out. This has been called 'the first mass movement of religious change backed by a new technology'. People of all sorts were in the game: famously Hans Sachs, Wagner's *Meistersinger*, along with less famous pamphleteers, furriers, bakers, weavers, gunsmiths, even women, although most were produced by humanists and clergy with more serious day-jobs, including Osiander, Amsdorf and Bucer. The most famous of the pamphlets was *Karsthans*, which epitomizes the perhaps deceptively demotic appeal of Protestantism. Karsthans ('Jack Hoe'), like the fourteenth-century English character Piers Plowman, is an honest tiller of the soil with little learning but much good sense.

Had the so-called 'peasants' who went on the rampage in 1525 read *Karsthans*? Were they perhaps a collectivity of Karsthanses? We have to be clear that the author of *Karsthans* was not a peasant but a learned classical scholar, who just may have been Vadianus (Joachim von Watt, 1484–1551), a native of St Gallen in Switzerland, rector of the University of Vienna and poet laureate to the Emperor Maximilian. Think of Pieter

Bruegel's *The Peasant Wedding*. This is not how peasants saw themselves, but how they were seen with some condescension by the artist and his patrons who were townsmen with money.

First, as we approach the Peasants' War, it is necessary to establish who were the actors: not peasants, if that suggests struggling subsistence farmers living on the edge, a Third World model. The kulaks of early twentieth-century Russia may be closer to the mark. And not peasants either if that suggests that the war was an entirely rural phenomenon. Miners and townspeople too were involved, and in some numbers. It is better to call this the Reformation of the People, or a rebellion of 'the common man'. But there was leadership, including that of clergy (Müntzer), other literate people and professional soldiers. Since our knowledge depends upon things that were written down we would like to know, but often cannot be certain, whether the ideas came from those who did the writing or whether they articulate a genuinely common mind.

Was the war about religion or politics, spiritual concerns or social justice? Similar questions have dominated discussion of the largest revolt against the Tudors, the Pilgrimage of Grace of 1536, and of the so-called Wars of Religion in France. Were they really about religion? And what about the civil wars in the British Isles in the mid-seventeenth century? Were they not also wars of religion? The answer may be that they were neither less nor more religious than those other wars of religion.

These questions have been badly put in so far as religious motives or 'factors' have been equated with, or measured against, other and more material concerns. If in 1525 religion appeared on shopping lists of grievances and demands, which is where we find it in the various 'articles' of groups of insurgent peasants, it also functioned more instrumentally, in three different ways: it was a precipitant; it was a binding force; and it provided legitimation.

This was not the first peasant revolt in late medieval Germany. Rather it was only the latest in a long run of rural disturbances, many of them adopting the symbol of the *Bundschuh*, or peasant laced boot. The peasants knew what it was to be, in the English idiom, 'up', which is to say, up in arms. However, this was a movement on a larger scale than anything seen before and it claimed a higher authority than any earlier uprising, no less an authority than God Almighty. It was now in the name of 'godly law' rather than 'ancient law', and with an appeal to scripture as the only true authority, that the peasants took to arms. They gave themselves names like 'Christian federation', 'Christian union', 'evangelical brotherly league'. In the manifesto known as the Twelve Articles, which has been called the 'conceptual glue' of the Peasants' War, the Upper Swabian peasants condemned serfdom as 'pitiable', 'for Christ has redeemed us all with the precious shedding of his blood, the lowly as well as the great'. The most militant of the peasant articles, drawn up near Schaffhausen on the Rhine, even declared that its authors had 'decided henceforth to have no lord but God alone'. Without Luther (and Zwingli, for Schaffhausen was in the orbit of the Swiss Reformation) this would not have happened.

Communal revolt, which may be regarded as dysfunctional, was an established tradition in the late medieval German countryside. But communalism itself was a growing functional factor. Peasants, too, had their politics and their own political consciousness. The village commune (*Gemeinde*), consisting of the more substantial householders (known in England as 'the better sort', the parish 'ancients') managed their own internal affairs, sometimes relatively free of the constraints of feudal lordship, in other circumstances in defiance of them. The competence to which they laid claim included matters of religion. The inhabitants of one Franconian village informed an incoming pastor in 1524 that they had the power to hire and fire him, that they regarded him as their servant ('we will give you orders'), and that if he failed to deliver the gospel 'in its purity' they would throw him out. Communality was an inherited value. But the notion of gospel purity was new and it both reinforced these communal values and turned them into a revolutionary cause. It was perhaps for that reason that the new evangelical religion was initially popular in many rural areas, especially in the south, from Alsace to Austria.

If communalism was growing, so were the contrary and often incompatible demands of the princes and other territorial lords, ratcheting up taxes and feudal dues, restricting access to common land and woodlands, denying the right to hunt and fish, operating the market to their own advantage, even, as the 'Articles of the Peasants of Stuhlingen' complained, appropriating public bathhouses 'which the commune built at its own expense'. This has been called the crisis of the agrarian order and the birthpangs of the early modern territorial state.

It all began in the region of the Black Forest and with such small-beer protests as refusing the feudal service of picking wild strawberries on a holiday. Like many popular disturbances in all parts of Europe, the beginnings were often carnivalesque and closer to 'industrial action' than war or revolution. The armed peasant bands roaming Upper Swabia in the early spring of 1525 said that they were exchanging Lenten cakes (pancakes). This was Shrovetide, a season for carnival and licensed misrule. (Rebellion in East Anglia in 1549 was referred to as the 'camping time'; camping was the local name for football, and the disturbances began as a kind of sport.)

What the peasants were up to soon became more serious than a game, and more threatening, with much of Germany engulfed, from Saxony to Swabia and the Tyrol (but not Bavaria and not the north-east). Carnival sometimes contained social conflict, but it could just as easily spill over. Bishops and monasteries were particular targets, with abbey after abbey sacked and burned, and the contents of their cellars drunk. For a time the insurgents were irresistible, the great powers of the Holy Roman Empire helpless. The city of Erfurt allowed the peasants in, partly out of fear, partly because they were a useful (and quite devastating) third force to use in the city's contention with the archbishop of Mainz. But in April and May 1525 the peasants were smashed by the forces of the Swabian League. This was not a foregone conclusion, not the outcome of what in the euphemism of today is called an 'asymmetrical' conflict. The peasants sometimes had superiority in numbers and they had both artillery and experienced mercenary officers, even if they lacked co-ordination. Those with a material interest in the status quo were entitled to be frightened.

Now, however, the princes would take over the Reformation and they would suppress the communal principle, while the Reformation of the People assumed the relatively apolitical form of Anabaptism, religion not a spur to direct action but a kind of sublimation and compensation. When the revolution of 1848 failed, Friedrich Engels thought that there were lessons to be learned from 1525. The rural population represented a force that in 1525 had almost succeeded and which the men of 1848 had been wrong to neglect. Peter Blickle, the leading historian of the Peasants' War and German communalism, called his book *The Revolution of 1525*. For him, this was quite simply 'the mightiest mass movement in European history before 1789'.

It is well known that in 1525 Luther wrote what he himself called a 'harsh' pamphlet: *Against the Robbing and Murdering Hordes of Peasants*. 'Let everyone who can, smite, slay, and stab.' When Luther wrote these words he was one of the frightened ones, not knowing that the rebels were going to lose. Soon he was widely criticized for showing no mercy to the now defeated peasants. But in an *Open Letter* he took nothing back. When the peasants were robbing, burning, plundering, who spoke of mercy then? 'Everything was "rights . . . Rights, rights, rights!"' 'You have to answer people like that with a fist . . . their ears must now be unbuttoned with musket balls till their heads jump off their shoulders.' There was a touch of even-handedness. If the lords were now misusing their power, they too would suffer. 'When I have time and occasion to do so, I shall attack the princes and lords too, for in my office of teacher, a prince is the same to me as a peasant.' (Somehow, he failed to get round to that.) Perhaps the most distasteful thing about these pamphlets is Luther's evident concern with his own reputation, which he seems to have cared about more than either princes or peasants.

What Luther could never forgive in the peasants was their wilful misunderstanding of what constituted Christian liberty, and indeed the claim that their cause was 'Christian'. Let them pursue their legitimate ends by legitimate means, but let them not call it Christian. That was to confuse the two kingdoms. 'There is nothing Christian on either side and nothing Christian is at issue between you.' That was Luther's interpretation of the Gospel. Was it the only valid or even the best interpretation? Blickle tells us that in a Zwinglian, south German context, 'the Revolution of 1525 was an unfolding of the Reformation itself'.

Only crass Marxists suppose that society is entirely about the distribution of goods and services, economics by another name.

People in the sixteenth century knew that it had to do with relationships, in the local community, but above all within the biological family: marriage, husbands and wives, parents and children. Women too were people, even if the sixteenth century accorded them limited legal rights and no public functions. We need to consider how far the Reformation made a difference to these fundamental building-blocks and nexuses of early modern European society. The answer may be not much. Votes for women was not yet a slogan. The nuclear family, parents and children, a patriarchal institution, was the Western European norm long before the sixteenth century and the century did nothing to change it. It may, however, have changed in important respects the way in which the institution experienced and expressed itself, which is not an easy subject for historians to handle. Was there such a thing as the Protestant family? Friedrich Engels thought so ('a conjugal partnership of leaden boredom, known as "domestic bliss"') – not that Engels knew much about it.

Yet again, we can start with Martin Luther. Luther's own marriage was the most notorious, most publicized marriage of the century, and he wrote extensively on the subject. Do we believe those social historians who assure us that the affectionate family had yet to be invented? This is what Luther wrote to his little son Hans: 'I know a beautiful garden, where there are many children with golden robes. They pick up the rosy-cheeked apples, pears, plums, etc., from under the trees, sing, jump, and rejoice all day long. They also have pretty ponies with golden reins and silver saddles.' Luther told Hans that he had asked the gardener whether Hans could come into the garden, eat the fruit, ride the ponies, play with the children. If he is good, said the gardener, he can, and Lippus and Jost too (sons of Luther's academic colleagues), 'and they shall get whistles and drums, and all sorts of musical instruments, and dance, and shoot with little cross-bows'. And could Aunt Lene come along? Of course. And this is what Luther wrote about his daughter Magdalena, who died in her teens: 'The tenderness of the father's heart is so great that we cannot think of it without sobs and sighs, which tear asunder the heart . . . You know how affectionate and sensible she was, nay, how charming.'

Luther had married Katharine von Bora when all the other nuns in her Wittenberg convent had already been snapped up. He said that his marriage had nothing to do with affection but was motivated by a sense of duty, not least to his father. It was also a matter of principle. Luther believed that marriage was both a divine imperative (God's first commandment was 'be fruitful and multiply') and a biological necessity as irresistible in all but very rare and exceptional cases as the urge to make water. It was not so much that sex was a good thing ('intercourse is never without sin') as that no one, certainly not 'religious' people, could claim exemption from the general state of sin of which it was a part. (Bucer and Calvin were more positive. A remedy for sin could not itself be a sin. Bucer also approved of divorce where pleasure and love had evaporated, a view that interested John Milton.) Luther's own marriage was successful, if adversarial. Katharine was his social superior (a *von* Bora) and had property of her own. Luther wrote from experience: 'There is no sweeter union than that in a good marriage. Nor is there any death more bitter than that which separates a married couple. Only the death of children comes close to this.' Katharine was to survive Martin but only to endure a miserable pillar-to-post life, and death, in the turmoil of the Schmalkaldic War and its aftermath.

If the Reformation made a difference, what was it? Did it offer women, even married women, a form of liberation? Or, on the contrary, did it tend to reinforce oppressive patriarchy? One book on the subject, by Steven Ozment, is called *When Fathers Ruled* (1983) and it concludes that paternal, husbandly rule was on the whole benign. Marriage was a refuge for women, if not for all women. Forty per cent were single, half of them spinsters, half widows. Women outside marriage were liable to be burned as witches. So did these single women benefit? At a time when the institution of marriage was conventionally denigrated the Reformation restored its dignity. Ozment thinks that there were worse fates in the sixteenth century than to be subject to a good man.

Lyndal Roper takes up a different position in a book with a title tinged with irony, *The Holy Household* (1989), as we might expect from acknowledgements that begin with tributes to the friendship and inspiration of the women's movement. Roper insists that the moral ethic of the Reformation, as studied in Augsburg, was 'a theology of gender'. To consider the effects of the Reformation beneficial for women was 'a profound misreading of the Reformation itself'. Women played a brief, transient role as Reformation agents. The few who had written pamphlets soon ceased to do so. There was 'a conservative shift' in the Reformation's message to women, as it 'reinscribed' women within the claustrophobic family. In the terms of Luther's Two Kingdoms Doctrine, men and women were spiritually equal but temporally unequal. Roper may remind us that the Ibsen who wrote *A Doll's House* was a Protestant.

Yet religion, and women were considered to be particularly good at it, provided them with space that might otherwise have been unavailable. Protestantism, like Catholicism, medieval and modern, furnishes remarkable examples of reciprocity and mutual dependence between men and women. John Knox, for all his public misogyny, revealed his inner self only to women who were ostensibly dependent upon his spiritual ministrations but on whom he also seems to have leant (unless this was no more than a cunning pastoral strategy). 'The exposition of your troubles and acknowledging of your infirmities were first unto me a very mirror and glass, wherein I beheld myself so richly painted forth, that nothing else could be more evident to my own eye': this to his mother-in-law.

We had better let Luther have the last word. His theology of gender was one of emancipation in a very limited, spiritual sense, just like his theology for the peasants. The option for a young woman of a celibate, religious life, which was sometimes a liberation, was now excluded, and good marriages were arranged marriages. But within marriage a Christian understanding of its value and meaning made all the difference. Washing a baby's nappies, smelling its stench, being kept awake all night by its crying: 'these are truly golden and noble works', and, it has to be said, for Luther they were chores fully shared by the father. His man was a new man. It is not difficult for an age thoroughly brainwashed by feminism and disposed to be cynical to dismiss this as so much holy hogwash. But it provides a good example of what Max Weber understood about the protestant doctrine of the calling (*Beruf*): how something as apparently conservative as the Protestant Ethic had the inner power to transform the world.

11 *Art*

'Is there in truth no beauty?' George Herbert's rhetorical question can serve as a response to the ignorant if understandable proposition that 'protestant art' is virtually an oxymoron. 'Truth', for Protestants, was biblical truth, and it was also 'the simple truth'. The beauty of true art lay in simplicity. That was an aesthetic that the Cistercian order had discovered long before in the austere chastity of their monastic churches. Go to Abbey Dore in Herefordshire where the remnants of the church, an auditorium these days for a music festival, retain their whitewashed Gothic verticality. Then cross the country to a greater Cistercian house, Fountains Abbey in Yorkshire, to observe that, artists being artists, and wealth being wealth, simple austerity often gives way to magnificence and decorative elaboration in spite of itself.

Protestants, as disciples of Erasmus and other humanists, were most at home when applying this aesthetic to verbal discourse. The English humanist, schoolmaster and dramatist Nicholas Udall (1505–56) wrote that while divinity 'loveth to be simple, so doth it not refuse eloquence, if the same come without injury or violation of the truth'. A 'plain style' such as Udall advocated eschewed 'elegancy of speech' but not eloquence. Udall was talking, proleptically, of the eloquence of *The Faerie Queene* and *Paradise Lost*. Defending 'the art of poetry', by which he meant fiction, as more informative than either philosophy or history, Sir Philip Sidney suggested that a man who had never seen a rhinoceros or an elephant had no need of a scientific treatise to know what the beast looked like if he could only be shown it 'well painted'. But Sidney was talking about poetry, not pictures. Poetry was a 'speaking picture': *'Ut pictura poesis'* (Horace, *Ars poetica*).

Sidney wrote that the Psalms of David make you 'as it were' see God in His majesty. Sidney knew that, according to John the Baptist (John 1:18), 'No man hath seen God at any time.' And he would not need to be reminded that God Himself through Moses had commanded: 'Thou shalt not make unto thee any graven image, or any likeness of any thing that is in heaven above, or that is in the earth beneath' (Exodus 20:4), words repeated in every church service. And yet the Reformation happened in a Europe where God the Father was not only painted in every church but impersonated in religious plays by your neighbour or the local butcher, baker or candlestick-maker. In the city of Chester it cost two pence 'for gilding of little God's face'.

What was the relation of pictures in the mind, formed by words, to images made concrete and visible on canvas or in stone or bronze, or even in the face-painting of a child? Erasmus had said that the New Testament made Jesus so fully present that you would see less if you were to gaze upon Him with your very eyes. But what did the child 'see' who had heard the Bible stories but had never gazed on pictures of Jesus such as later generations of Sunday School children would be exposed to? Not even the contorted figure on the cross was readily envisaged, since English Protestants did all they could to banish crosses not only from churches but from the landscape and even as items of personal adornment. Did protestant iconoclasts who attacked sacred images, verbally or physically, approve or disapprove of images in the mind? On this crucial issue there was much perplexity. Another poet of the age, John Donne, admitted: 'To adore, or scorn an image, or protest / May all be bad.'

Iconoclasm, hostility to false images, is where any account of Protestantism and art has to begin. The sixteenth century witnessed a holocaust of religious imagery, the most extensive and thorough in history. So efficiently did the Elizabethans eradicate the life-sized figures of Christ on the cross (or 'rood', hence 'rood screen'), flanked by images of Mary and John, which had commanded the devotion of the worshippers in every parish church, that today only one set of pre-Reformation images survives, in a small church in Wales.

The Lutheran strand in Protestantism was to be the least iconoclastic of all protestant traditions, yet it was in Luther's Wittenberg, in the Movement of 1521-2, that Reformation iconoclasm had its first recorded origins. In *On the abolishing of images* (1522) that original if muddled man Andreas Bodenstein von Karlstadt rationalized the destruction of religious imagery, revealing something of the psychology and motivation of the iconoclast. 'My heart since childhood has been brought up in the veneration of images, and a harmful fear has entered me which I gladly would rid myself of, and cannot.' Forbidden fruit! The iconoclast is not colour-blind or tone-deaf when it comes to images. He loves them too much, so much that he needs to destroy them, and so to destroy the images in his mind and heart.

It may be because Luther was not so strongly attached to images that he came to regard them, and the appeal they had for ordinary Christians, with relative complacency. The great Nuremberg churches of St Sebald and St Lawrence remain showcases for the glories of late medieval and Renaissance art. Luther thought that people should be allowed such things, as children are allowed their toys. Karlstadt believed that that was like letting a child play with a sharp-pointed knife. 'We should take such horrible things from the weak, and snatch them from their hands.' Even the moderate Melanchthon was for a time impressed by Karlstadt's argument and by the preaching of another of Luther's more impassioned colleagues, Gabriel Zwilling (1487–1558). Zwilling personally burned pictures and altarpieces, encouraging the students and townspeople who engaged in an orgy of destruction which Luther denounced on his return from the Wartburg.

Iconoclasm was transient and peripheral to the Lutheran Reformation, if not to the street theatre and politics of some of the German people. But it was integral to Zwingli's Swiss Reformation. Zwingli rejected church music, 'which not the hundredth part understands', the uncomprehending mumbling of the Psalms by nuns, those 'singing fools'. This was the attitude of an exceptionally sensitive musician, trained to a high standard, who knew the power of music, thoroughly approved of its secular use, and even composed a four-part battle song for the war in which he lost his life. But, like Karlstadt, where the things of God were concerned Zwingli was a total rejectionist. Other reformers, including Oecolampadius in Basle, tried to persuade him of the merits of congregational singing. Zwingli was unmoved and worship in Zürich took place in a still silence, like that of a Quaker meeting, but only until 1598, when singing was restored, literally over what was left of Zwingli's dead body.

Those same scriptural principles were brought to bear on religious imagery. Zürich had recently experienced an unprecedented explosion of artistic activity in which the Church had shared, a time of conspicuous consumption paid for by the mercenary business. Not that Zürich art, any more than its music, was very good or anything more than provincial. It was quantity rather than quality, a painted altarpiece for every one of the city's hundred altars, seventeen of them in the Gross Münster alone. This was religion mediated through sense, especially the sense of sight. On Ascension Day in Zürich a huge image of Christ was actually hoisted out of the floor by a machine and up through a hole in the roof made for the purpose.

Zwingli totally rejected sensuous religion, insisting that the God who was an invisible, intangible spirit must be worshipped spiritually. Therefore he could not accept the real presence in the sacrament. Surprisingly, since Zwingli had always denounced the veneration of saints, it was not until 1523 that any attempt was made to remove the images of saints from the Zürich churches. It was then that an inflammatory sermon (not preached by Zwingli), followed by a very few isolated incidents and a series of consequential debates, led the great council of the city, advised by Zwingli and a special committee, to settle the matter legally. 'Images and idols' were to be done away with, but 'with good behaviour', not 'wantonly'. At midsummer in 1524, clergy, committee men, police, together with the city architect, stonemasons, carpenters and other workmen entered every church, locked the doors behind them, and proceeded to dismantle everything in sight. Standing statues and their niches and bases were removed. Painted altarpieces were burned outside. Murals were chipped and scraped off the walls. It took thirteen days. One pious citizen, a veteran of pilgrimage, found the result 'hideous'. Zwingli exulted: 'The walls are beautifully white!' Music (even religious music) and the visual arts were by no means extinguished, but they now happened in the homes of wealthy burghers; portraits of real people, 'living images made by God', replaced the man-made pictures of saints.

Iconoclasm was a more tumultuous affair in other places,

including Basle, where image-breaking riots involved thousands of people and brought the city to the brink of insurrection. The funeral pyres of debris from the devastated cathedral and other churches burned for two days and nights, a sad experience for the now elderly Erasmus. However, the Zürich example was normative, especially in its orderliness, and it may well have been consciously followed in England in the summer of 1559 when the new Elizabethan regime, in the shape of commissioners some of whom had just returned from Zürich, purged the churches of 'monuments of idolatry', but without any riotous demonstrations.

Zwinglianism chimed in with an ancient tradition of English heretical sentiment, hostility to images having been a hallmark of Lollardry. It was said that Lollards condemned the arts of painting and engraving as 'generally superfluous and naught, and against God's Laws'. The objects they physically assaulted were invariably three-dimensional, sculpted and painted images. Here was a significant conjunction of the old heresy and the new. When in the 1520s the pioneering Cambridge reformer Thomas Bilney preached at Willesden, a famous Marian shrine, he told his congregation to 'put away your golden gods, your silver gods, your stony gods,' and told an unlikely tale about priests taking the jewels off images, hanging them around the necks of their whores, and then putting them back on the images. When Bilney was burned at the stake in Norwich four men walked twenty miles through the night to burn the famous rood of Dovercourt in Essex, a symbolic act of defiant revenge.

This was one reason why Zwinglian (or Reformed) Protestantism won out in England over the more conservative Lutheranism. Queen Elizabeth I was the exception to prove this rule. She was a Lutheran in so far as she made a distinction between images (good) and idols (bad), and continued to venerate the cross. Lutherans, like Catholics, conflated what we know as the first and second of the Ten Commandments, the effect of which was to treat the second admonition, 'Thou shalt not make unto thee any graven image,' as a mere gloss on the first, 'Thou shalt have no other gods before me.' That was to outlaw idols but not necessarily images. However, for Elizabeth's bishops, who belonged to the Zwinglian tradition in this respect, the second commandment was free-standing and absolute within itself. They told the queen that 'if by virtue of the second commandment images were not lawful in the temple of the Jews, then by the same commandment they are not lawful in the churches of Christians'. Elizabeth, rather grudgingly, preferred to say that there should be no images 'for fear and occasion of worshipping them, though they be of themselves indifferent', and continued to pray in front of a crucifix in her own chapel.

Everywhere there was interplay between popular, disorderly and illegal iconoclasm and the legal kind, ordered and overseen by the civil authorities. The wanton, unauthorized destruction of images was a very serious offence, only a little less so if the destroyer of the image was the man who had set it up in the first place and whose property in some sense it still was. When a farmer in Zwingli's native Toggenburg mutilated a painting of the crucifixion in a pub, saying that 'images are useless . . . and of no help', he was executed. Three of the four Dovercourt iconoclasts were hanged. However, as with bible translation and dissemination, the distinction was often blurred. In the secondary wave of iconoclasm that hit England in the revolution of the 1640s, William Dowsing travelled throughout Cambridgeshire and East Anglia removing and breaking down many of the images that had survived the Reformation. Dowsing was duly commissioned to do what he did, but he was responsible for obtaining the commission and he put it into execution with an enthusiasm that was self-motivated.

It was in 1538 that Henry VIII and his first minister Thomas Cromwell made iconoclasm government policy. Images of the Virgin from Walsingham and Ipswich were publicly burned, while the celebrated rood of the Cistercian abbey of Boxley (in Kent), which turned its head, rolled its eyes and moved its lips (in the words of a contemporary ballad, 'he was made to joggle, / his eyes would goggle'), was hawked around the country before being burned at a ceremony at Paul's Cross in London. A report of this was sent to Bullinger in Zürich. In the same year a Franciscan friar whose 'heresy' was to believe in the pope was roasted alive in Smithfield over a fire made from the famous Welsh image of Dderfel Gadarn, which had attracted pilgrims in their hundreds, relying on the saint to get them out of hell if by any chance they should be damned. (However, the wooden horse on which the saint had been mounted remained in Merioneth for centuries, an object of veneration in the absence of its rider.) On the night of Friar Forest's incineration the miracle-working Rood of Grace in the London church of St Margaret's Pattens was smashed to pieces by 'certain lewd persons' of the parish, an unlawful act. But the killing of two birds with one stone by burning the friar and the image of the saint was lawful, indeed a piece of government propaganda, helping justify the king's proceedings in banishing the pope and dissolving the monasteries. The key word in both cases was 'feigned': feigned religion, false art.

The most dramatic episode of iconoclasm of a popular, even revolutionary character happened in the Netherlands in the 'Wonderyear' of 1566. It was in the summer of 1566 that the Dutch Calvinists, who had been meeting in secret conventicles, came out into the open in so-called 'hedge-preachings' which drew crowds of twenty-five thousand to the fields outside Antwerp. Pieter Bruegel recorded the scene in his *The Sermon of Saint John the Baptist*, a mixed crowd in a landscape looking nothing like the Jordan Valley, tightly packed together, perched in trees. The next logical step was for the artisans who had come out to hear the hedge-preachers to take forceful possession of the cities and their churches, and this offensive was spearheaded by a wave of iconoclastic outrages which began in West Flanders on 10 August and spread to all seventeen provinces in less than two weeks. In Antwerp thirty churches were sacked in two days (20–21 August) while the citizen guard looked the other way. On the 22nd it was the turn of Ghent. Images were not just destroyed, they were tortured, eyes gouged out and faces mutilated, heads cut off in mock executions. (Jan van Eyck's great altarpiece, *The Adoration of the Lamb*, was rescued by the family of its donors.) When asked who had given them authority to commit such deeds some of the iconoclasts answered, 'God.'

The meaning of iconoclasm, not so much the one-off events as the mass movements of the kind seen in Flanders and Brabant in 1566, is one of those questions that gives employment to social and cultural as well as religious historians. Was iconoclasm wholly spontaneous and in that sense 'popular', or were the iconoclasts manipulated by the preachers and other 'leaders'? Were these examples of displaced aggression? Were the 'real' targets the clergy or the hated Spanish regime? Luther knew that there was not a huge difference between annihilating images and killing people. The Old Testament sentence against idolaters was death. Iconoclasm led on to rebellion, just as the storming of the Bastille was the overture to the French Revolution. The Wonderyear was a year of unemployment, a hungry year. But explanations along Marxist lines will probably not suffice. Some such motives as Karlstadt articulated may have operated at a deeper level. To destroy the object of belief was to blot out the belief itself. The image of the saint *was* the saint, just as the face on the television screen is the virtual reality. To break the holy image, to smash the screen, was to break the holy power. All idols, it might be said, have feet of clay.

Do we need to say that the iconoclasts did not consider, or even know, that what they were attacking were works of art? 'Art' in our sense was not the issue, there being no 'art for art's sake'. However, returning to our sense of what constitutes art, what did the Reformation put in the place of the gilded images of saints? When the court musician Thomas Sternhold (d. 1549) invited the boy king Edward VI to become a patron of the new fashion of singing 'scripture songs', exchanging 'feigned rhymes of vanity' for 'holy songs of verity', he did not ask him to alter his musical taste since Sternhold's Psalms were composed in the style of lute songs. Only the words were different. On the other hand, in Scotland the Reformation obliged leading composers to abandon polyphony and, whether they liked it or not, to compose metrical psalm tunes conforming to the rule of one word, one note. The greatest English composer of the age, Thomas Tallis (1510?–85), also had to adapt but not so drastically, while his pupil William Byrd (1543–1623), the greatest name in the next generation, pursued am amphibious career as a 'church papist' writing for both the English catholic community and the Chapel Royal.

How far were artists likewise constrained to change the styles in which they painted? Did they themselves undergo conversions which we can find reflected in their work? We know that Vermeer had his 'periods', dictated by the religious environment in which he found himself. When in 1653 he married a catholic wife, converted to Catholicism and kept house with his wealthy mother-in-law, he painted in the Caravaggio-like style of Catholic Utrecht. His more familiar domestic scenes, however, are suffused with a light that is surely both protestant and secular, pure Delft, but Delft transcended, Vermeer being Vermeer.

Once again, we have to distinguish between the Lutheran and Reformed (Zwinglian) traditions. In Lutheran Germany religious change redirected the activity of artists without suppressing it. This is copiously documented in the evolving work of Luther's close friend Lucas Cranach the Elder (1472–1553), who in 1529 produced what has been called 'the quintessential Reformation image', a theologically didactic *Allegory of Law and Grace*, which was painted on panels, published as a woodcut, and widely copied. Cranach has been called 'Reformation art in mass production', and he did very well out of the business, building one of the most handsome houses in Wittenberg (which still exists). He and his son, Lucas Cranach the Younger (1515–86) were responsible for those portraits of Luther (and other members of his family), Melanchthon and other reformers that have fixed them for ever in our mind's eye.

What of the greatest artist of his time in northern Europe, Albrecht Dürer (1471–1528)? Dürer had made his name and fortune with spectacular woodcut albums of religious subjects such as the *Apocalypse* (1498) and the *Passion* (1511). These works, for which the patron was the public, an important moment in art history, are the most eloquent expressions still available to us of the intense Christocentrism and religious anxieties of Luther's generation. Dürer was powerfully affected by Luther, describing him as 'a Christian man who helped me out of great distress'. When, after Worms, he believed that Luther might have been killed, Dürer poured out his anguish:

'Oh God, if Luther is dead, who will ever expound the gospel to us with such clarity?' But whether Dürer should be called a protestant artist is another, and probably anachronistic, question.

Dürer's great painting of the *Four Apostles*, which he presented to the city fathers of Nuremberg, his native city, in 1526 is a monument both to protestant biblicism and to post-1525 conservatism. It depicts on two panels the larger-than-life figures of St John and St Peter, St Paul and St Mark. St Paul is carrying a huge bible while St Peter, who is equipped with his key but is a distinctly subordinate figure, is looking down on the text of St John's Gospel, opened by John himself, on which Dürer has inscribed the opening words in Luther's concise version: *'Im Anfang war das Wort'* ('In the beginning was the Word'). If the images of saints had formerly been the objects of the worshipper's gaze, it is now St Paul who, with an almost menacing sideways look, is fixing his eye on the viewer. Beneath the painting there are scriptural quotations from the four biblical authors, all supportive of Christian magistracy and admonishing 'all worldly rulers in these dangerous times': 'Hear therefore these four excellent men, Peter, John, Paul, and Mark, their warning.' The work may have begun life as an intended altarpiece but it now had nowhere to go but into the grateful hands of the secular rulers of the city. According to one critic, Dürer was expressing his disillusionment with a Reformation that had proved a moral failure. Perhaps. But for our purposes the painting can stand as testimony to his belief in the validity of religious art as, in his own words, doing more good than harm 'when it is honourably, artistically, and well made'. However, Dürer died in 1528 and the decades that followed witnessed a dramatic decline in the quantity and quality of German artistic production, which may or may not be attributable to the Reformation.

Meanwhile, in England, the German artist Hans Holbein the Younger (1498–1543) had no opportunities to produce religious art. He had witnessed the destruction of the great altarpiece that his father had erected for the St Moritzkirche in Augsburg, and in the 1520s he himself painted altarpieces in Lucerne and Basle. He came to England in the aftermath of the iconoclastic holocaust in Basle, recommended by Erasmus in a letter that spoke of the arts freezing in that city. It was out of the fridge and into the freezer. Holbein now made a new career as a portrait artist. It says everything about the nature of the English Reformation that he was now to paint not saints but Henry VIII, in various versions of the truly monstrous, statuesque portrait by which everyone still remembers him. The religious character of the Henrician Reformation, however, is best conveyed in Holbein's engraved title page for the Great Bible, which is about biblical religion but above all about obedience. It is the king who is made virtually the author of the sacred text as, in a parody of conventional representations of donor and patron, he hands the Bible to representative leaders of Church and State, and so on down to the common people, who respond with glad cries of 'Vivat Rex', 'God Save the King'.

In Reformed territories, and we may take England as a convenient example, there was a creeping retreat from the artistic treatment of religion that at its extremity led to something beyond iconoclasm: iconophobia of the kind we otherwise associate with Wahhabite Islam. It was an agonizing time for the naturally iconophile. When the artistically gifted Richard Haydocke translated the Italian treatise by Giovanni Paolo Lomazzo, *Trattato dell'Arte* (*A tracte containing the artes of curious paintinge*, 1598), the bible of mannerist artists, he added to the recommendation that God the Father ought to be painted only with 'perfect colours', 'And I think he should not be painted at all.'

However, the story of the visual arts in the Calvinist Reformation is more complicated than one of simple and progressive decline. Lyon as a (briefly) protestant city cornered the market in illustrated bibles, while the print trade along what has been called the Lyon–Geneva axis was capable of producing visual images of high technical proficiency. In about 1566 a *Mappemonde nouvelle papistique* was published, a stunning engraving that showed catholic Europe caught up in the tentacles of a huge and beautifully depicted protestant octopus. This, however, was very much the exception to prove the rule that Calvinist books applied the second commandment very liberally, eschewing for the most part pictures of any kind.

In England, in what may be called the initial Reformation, the visual arts were deployed to devastating effect against the pope and other symbols of unreformed religion. A number of pictures and woodcut book illustrations depict the pope tumbling down and losing his tiara or making a convenient footstool for the godly monarch. Images of emperors and kings on their knees before popes and papal legates, kissing the papal foot, surrendering their crowns, were deployed as almost pornographic parodies of traditional representations of the Magi kneeling at the feet of Christ. This tradition had a long future. As a new national memory became stocked with examples of Catholic aggression and subversion, such as the Armada and Guy Fawkes, stock images were produced well into the seventeenth century, not only in woodcuts and engravings but in embroidery. However, this was anti-Catholic rather than Protestant art.

Many mid-sixteenth-century English bibles were copiously

illustrated, although the Geneva Bible (1560) restricted itself to maps and other strictly informative graphics. Every edition of John Foxe's 'Book of Martyrs', from 1563 onwards, was enlivened with pictures that were to have at least as much impact as the text on many generations of readers: stoical martyrs in flaming agony; Bishop Bonner caning the bare backside of a protestant prisoner in his orchard, bursting out of a rather too tight codpiece. In the copy of the 1570 edition in the Cambridge University Library the pictures are coloured, and there is evidence that they were sometimes detached and stuck on walls.

England, a cultural backwater, lacked the expertise and technical capacity to produce printed pictures on anything like the German scale. In the late 1560s a Huguenot refugee called Giles Godet published and marketed in London highly sophisticated albums of biblical prints in the Parisian style, sequences of the Creation, the life of Joseph, the story of the prodigal son, employing children to colour them in and selling them at one penny plain, twopence coloured. For the English market pictures of God the Father were omitted. All this belonged to an early protestant aesthetic the concomitants of which were plays, both scriptural and anti-Catholic, and psalms and other 'godly' ballads sung to popular tunes and peddled by the balladsellers. The traditional media were not jettisoned but appropriated. We may call this phase iconoclastic rather than iconophobic, since there was a rejection not of art as such, not even religious art, but of false, deceitful, popish art.

However, Godet died in 1571 and had no successor. From about this time English bibles were no longer illustrated. It is unlikely that Foxe's pictures would have been commissioned if his 'Book of Martyrs' had been published for the first time in the 1580s. The year 1580 registers a general cultural shift, which included the growth of a strong anti-theatrical prejudice. Religious plays were said to be the worst of all. Christ had not been born to be 'played' on a stage, and indeed after about 1580 He would not appear there again until the twentieth century. It was no longer thought appropriate to sing the psalms to popular tunes like 'Greensleeves', and the fashion for producing godly parodies of secular ballads fell away. As for religious pictures, they were suspicious evidence of popery if found on the person or in some private place. One of the most trendy of literary genres was now the collection of 'emblems', normally consisting of a picture, a verse and an adage, mutually but cryptically interpretative. But there were even such things as 'blind' emblem books, without pictures. The cultural shift can be overstated. The 'idolatrous' eye and its object may have been suspect but Elizabethan and Jacobean walls were hung with painted cloths, tapestries if you could afford them, and inns and taverns were decorated with pictures of the prodigal son as well as the terse admonition 'Fear God'.

But in so far as art experienced a secular displacement, this was perhaps an emancipation. Once again, the theatre offers a parallel. The passing of the old moralities and mystery plays, even in their short-lived protestant forms, opened the way for the rich repertoire of the late Elizabethan and Jacobean theatre, which included plays like *Measure for Measure* that handled 'morality' at a more profound level.

So it was that the visual arts came to concentrate on human individuality, both the painted portrait and tomb sculptures. Sadly for the English social and cultural historian, it is necessary to cross the North Sea to discover the full potential of protestant art as it reproduced the streets and marketplaces, the taverns and intimate interiors of seventeenth-century Holland, not forgetting those many painterly visions of the luminous interior of the Nieuwe Kerk in Delft, the tomb of William the Silent seen from every possible angle. It encapsulates the story of art in the Reformation that painters now found employment in painting pretty pictures of churches rather than in painting images for the Church.

12 A Reformation watershed?

My five-year-old son, standing in front of a newly acquired picture hung on the wall while he slept, a sad, unpopulated landscape, asked: 'Did that happen a long time ago, and are all the people dead?' It did, and they are. When little Wilhelmine and Peterkin in Robert Southey's poem pestered Old Kaspar with questions about the Battle of Blenheim, 'Now tell us all about the war, / And what they fought each other for', 'What good came of it at last?', he could not remember. 'But 'twas a famous victory.' We may now have some sense of what Protestants and Catholics fought each other for. What good came of it at last is not for the historian to say. But whether anything ultimately significant came of it is a question that we cannot so easily dodge.

Everything is the cause of everything. The historian is not a scientist in a laboratory, where agents and catalysts can be isolated and tested against control experiments, but an artist confronting the whole messy world, a vast landscape of contingency. It is inevitable that something as large as the Reformation should have been made the cause of many things. And since 'the Reformation' is, if not a figment, a construction of the historical imagination, we can make it the cause of almost as much as we want. It was, perhaps, a precondition (along with what else?) for that other watershed in our civilization, that other construction, the Enlightenment. If the Reformation represented an emancipation of the mind and the untrammelled communication of knowledge, which was not at all what Luther and Calvin intended, then it was equally a precondition for what has been labelled the Scientific Revolution. Would Europe have given the world Newton, or Darwin, without the Reformation? We will never know. But we do know that the Catholic Church condemned Galileo, and with Galileo the Copernican doctrine of the circulation of the planets around the sun, and that it was only in 1992 that Pope John Paul II admitted that that had been a mistake – which is not to say that most Protestants would have given Galileo the thumbs-up, any more than in 1859 (or in the American Midwest into the twenty-first century) they would allow Darwin's *Origin of Species* to be even plausibly true.

The Reformation (and Counter-Reformation) was the blast furnace in which the modern state was forged. Wars of religion and the secular appropriation of ecclesiastical powers and property facilitated the process of state-building. A Europe at peace in the two centuries that followed the Reformation is hard to imagine: Germany without the Thirty Years' War; Britain and France lying down together like the lion and the lamb. The essentially Protestant state of Great Britain, the state that celebrated itself in 'Rule Britannia!', imagined and realized itself in more than a century of wars with the French, which were not without ideology even if they were wars of empire rather than of religion.

Late nineteenth-century Germany, the Bismarckian Reich, saw a titanic struggle, the *Kulturkampf*, to determine whether Catholicism could be a stakeholder within it. The Spanish–American War of 1898 was seen by Protestants as a struggle between two versions of civilization, its outcome not in doubt. The papal Syllabus of Errors (1864), eighty of them, concluded with condemnation of the proposition that the supreme pontiff 'can and ought to reconcile and adjust himself with progress, liberalism, and modern civilization': something like a suicide note, for surely those things were bound to prevail? In France, leading politicians of the Third Republic supposed that their main task was to overcome something called 'clericalism', which meant religion, and which required the adoption of the American, and protestant, principle of the dissociation of Church and state. The post-Second World War phenomenon of Christian Democracy was a rather late concession by Catholicism to the politics of the modern world.

Midwives are not needed when children begin to grow up. It is now inconceivable that religion could play a major part in a British general election such as it did in 1906. In the British Isles, and outside Northern Ireland, religion remains an issue only to the limited extent that politics are about morality: the politics of 'life issues'. The workings of the European Union, its possible expansion, the merits or otherwise of a single currency, economic globalization and the role of multinational companies are matters without even so much as a religious tincture. But has this very secularization of politics been a delayed consequence of the Reformation?

Even more problematical are the ideas about Protestantism and modernization advanced by one of the most powerful and open minds to apply itself to what has been called 'the miracle of the West', that of the German sociologist Max Weber. According to Weber, Protestantism had something to do with the 'rise' of capitalism and its concomitant, industrial civilization. The debate over whether the Reformation in its office of midwife functioned positively, providing an ethical motive for the accumulation of wealth on an unprecedented scale, or negatively, by removing the ecclesiastical constraints on capitalist enterprise that we associate with the Middle Ages, which was the version of the story favoured by the English Christian Socialist R. H. Tawney in his *Religion and the Rise of Capitalism* (1926), was one that never took place because Tawney supposed, mistakenly, that he and Weber were saying the same thing; and Weber was dead before Tawney put pen to paper.

Few theories have been more widely misunderstood than the thesis advanced in Weber's *The Protestant Ethic and the Spirit of Capitalism* (1905). Sir Geoffrey Elton wrote of his 'sadness', 'sadness at so much misguided effort, and sadness at the willingness of historians to worship the graven image set up by the sociologists', while A. G. Dickens thought that 'nowadays no one has a kind word for Max Weber's thesis', which he called a 'specious theory'. It is clear that these two leading, utterly empirical, British historians had little idea what Weber was going on about.

There are those who have said that Weber only had himself to blame. But Weber could not have made clearer what he was and was not proposing about the connections between Protestantism, and especially Calvinism, and what he called 'the spirit of capitalism'. It was not, he insisted, his aim to substitute for a one-sided materialistic causal interpretation of culture and history (in short, Marxism) an equally one-sided spiritualistic interpretation. 'Each is equally possible, but each, if it does not serve as the preparation, but as the conclusion of an investigation, accomplishes equally little in the interest of historical truth.' Almost his last written words were to say that that should have been that.

To understand Weber it is necessary to penetrate his philosophy of causation. That is a rather complicated matter, but he certainly did not suggest that Calvinism 'caused' the phenomenon of modern capitalism in any simple sense. It is also helpful to know where Weber was coming from. It is the crassest of mistakes to suppose that he invented the linkage between religion and society or, more specifically, between Protestantism and progress. The relative success of the Protestant states of north-west Europe, especially Britain and Holland, was a matter much discussed in the eighteenth century. That protestant individuals and societies do better than Catholics was something that everyone in Weber's Germany thought they knew. Catholics themselves believed that they suffered from an intellectual and cultural 'deficit'. What was novel about the late nineteenth century was that Marxists and other anti-religious materialists denied or played down the social significance of religion.

What all social historians of the Reformation, and indeed of religion in general, owe to Weber is a principle rather clumsily translated into English from an even more cumbersome German original as 'elective affinity', otherwise described as 'certain correlations between forms of religious belief and practical ethics'. This was something different from the exact equation of religious ideas and social forces that Marxists had proposed, but was more of a modification than a contradiction since Weber too was a kind of Marxist. Religious ideas come from nowhere, or from nowhere accessible to the social scientist: the myth of the Old Testament prophet, or of Martin Luther. Once launched, however, their trajectory is determined by the material and psychological needs of the individuals and groups who are their recipients and vectors. Religious believers and practitioners select out from the entirety of the religious message elements that are relevant to their needs, or seem to be so. Ideas alone are useless for any social purpose unless they have some sort of practical outcome, but they can operate like points on a railway track redirecting action that is driven by the dynamics of interest. 'Material without ideal interests are empty, but ideals without material interests are impotent.' This is a very important statement. So it was that the acute religious anxiety that Weber believed, rightly or wrongly, to have been the typical mental and spiritual state of the devout Calvinist (and he really had very little means of knowing about that) came to have something to do with successful entrepreneurship.

However, Weber, no less than Marx, did not merely want to understand such things. He wanted to change them, and his famous essay has been called 'an allegory about Germany in his own day' written by a would-be Englishman. For the Protestantism that Weber believed to be a dynamic force having a close affinity, to say no more, with 'the spirit of capitalism', was not the stultifying Lutheran orthodoxy of Wilhelm II's authoritarian Germany but the Protestantism of Manchester and America with its values of self-determining, nonconformist individualism and independence: an Atlantic Protestantism of Puritanism and Dissent.

Weber has helped us to see that the legacy of the Reformation was two very different Protestantisms. These were not so much the theologically and institutionally distinct Lutheran and Calvinist traditions, although those were locked in mortal combat in Germany towards 1600, as what a historian of French Protestantism has called *l'établissement* (whether Evangelical or Reformed) contrasted with a succession of renewals of the Reformation, self-conscious reformations of the Reformation, outside the establishment and even against it. In England this latter Protestantism achieved a capital N: Nonconformity of various kinds. Who invented chocolate? The English Nonconformists called Quakers. Religious revolutions are like the lava flow from an intermittently active volcano. The magma cools and sets in solid rock formations only for the fissures to open again to renew the process. The Quakers were a new Reformation.

German historians in particular have identified a phase of post-Reformation history sometimes called 'confessionalization' and, where Calvinism replaced an earlier Lutheranism, the Second Reformation. Theologically, the Second Reformation applies not so much to Calvin, who in many respects we may regard as a primary reformer, as to the post-Calvin generation of Beza, the Heidelberg theologians and, in England, William Perkins (1558–1602). It was a neo-scholastic Protestantism which made a science out of the business of being saved, with the Bible as not so much a collection of salvation stories as a technical handbook to be interpreted with the aid of the schematic tools provided by the French logician Peter Ramus (Pierre de la Ramée, 1515–72), who lost his life in the St Bartholomew massacre. Now *sola scriptura* meant not so much the whole thrust of the biblical message as the import of this or that text, chapter and verse, properly expounded.

This was a developmental stage marked by the hardening of doctrine into those tablets of stone that were the various Protestant confessions of faith, not without much theological infighting, whether between Gnesio-Lutherans and Melanchthonian Lutherans (Philippists), or between Remonstrants and Contraremonstrants in Holland, or involving various kinds of Calvinists in the French protestant academies. The Catholic Church of the Counter-Reformation was subject to the same process, for the Canons and Decrees of Trent were far from the last word. For many years a special congregation in Rome, the Congregatio de Auxiliis, debated the same issue that divided Calvinists, the manner in which divine grace operates, only for the matter to be adjourned to seventeenth-century France where the Jansenists would do battle with the Jesuits. The twin processes of polarization and solidification went together and interacted, and what neither made any allowance for was the sturdy individualism that Weber believed to be the true spirit of Protestantism.

For another aspect of confessionalization was the ever stricter control of the beliefs and moral conduct of the subjects of princes and other governments that adopted one or another of the new orthodoxies, a repressive if creative alliance of secular and clerical power. That in turn was an important part of the process of state-building, especially in the German principalities. Once again, this was cross-confessional. There was no more resolute confessional absolutist than the emperor Ferdinand II, who shared responsibility with the Calvinist elector palatine Frederick V (disastrously elected king of Bohemia in 1619) for the Thirty Years' War. One of the few benefits to come out of that almost genocidal conflict and the Peace of Westphalia which ended it (in 1648) was the partial submergence of Evangelical–Reformed animosities in a common protestant cause.

In spite of its semi-toleration of religious minorities, Georgian England was another example of the confessional state. In the preceding century the processes of confessionalization had been hotly contested. What was 'orthodoxy'? Churchmen of various tendencies jockeyed for position and for the right to say what it was. When kings made themselves the ultimate arbiters and pursued unpopular religious policies they were deposed, even decapitated. As for the Second Reformation, its place was taken by the incessant demand of the Puritans for what they called 'Further Reformation'. The frustration of this cause from generation to generation, especially in the 1630s, a decade dominated by the reactionary, almost anti-protestant regime of

Archbishop William Laud (1573–1645), became so acute that it provoked a true Second Reformation, a replay, existentially, of the first and with much wider popular support. In 1641 John Milton published a tract *Of Reformation in England and the causes that hitherto have hindred it.* In the 1670s and 1680s, the whole film was played over again, minus the civil war bits. Even in the 1690s, under the rule of William and Mary, which was validated by their Protestantism, there was the feel of a new reformation, especially of 'manners'. The English Reformation was a very long reformation indeed. Out of it came the kind of Protestantism for which Max Weber hankered.

In the German heartland of the Reformation, much of it a wasteland in the aftermath of the most serious war so far in European history, there was a second reformation spring in the movement known as Pietism, a response to the era of orthodoxy through a renewed cultivation of the religious inner life, a reaction against arid formalism driven by the conviction that Christianity is a way of life, something to be done rather than learned. Most English Christians are familiar with the hymn 'O sacred head, sore wounded', its tune elaborated by Bach through the passions and cantatas, and they might guess that it was written by Luther himself. In fact, the author was Paul Gerhardt (1607–76), his bitter experience in the Thirty Years' War refracted in its verses: confessional Lutheranism rather than Pietism but with embers aglow that would soon burst into Pietist flame.

The Englishman John Wesley (1703–91), on his way to America as a missionary and still before his evangelical conversion, taught himself German by translating Gerhardt's hymns. Pietism crossed, as it were, the spark gap of the linguistic divide to ignite the great Evangelical Awakening that in the eighteenth century gave birth to Wesley's Methodism and to a wider, indeed truly ecumenical, Evangelical Movement which spanned the Atlantic, energized humanitarian responses to the wars and other catastrophes of the age, abolished slavery, and sent missionaries into Africa. The liberator William Wilberforce (1759–1833) wrote a manifesto for Evangelicalism: his *Practical View of the Prevailing Religious System of Professed Christians* (1797). It was this that made the Victorians serious.

For many neglected corners, what seventeenth-century Puritans had called 'the dark corners of the land', Evangelicalism, which ignored denominational frontiers, was the only authentic reformation. Out of all this came a series of 'revivals' in the later eighteenth and nineteenth centuries, beginning with the American 'Great Awakening' of the 1740s inspired by Jonathan Edwards (1703–58). These were the remote precursors of the industrialized tele-evangelism of more recent times. Wales was subjected to a hurricane of revival as late as 1905, and there were more revivals in the Western Isles of Scotland up to the middle years of the twentieth century. Since then the Spirit, which bloweth where it listeth, has not listed to blow, which is as much as to say that most of Britain is now post-Christian.

I am not sure that we have yet attempted to cross the bridge, if it exists, that connects the world of the Reformation to the modern world. It may be, in essence, a question of whether Christian belief was universal in the sixteenth century, as it surely was not a few centuries later. Was the old world of Christendom still intact if fragmented? In a famous book, *The Problem of Unbelief in the Sixteenth Century: the Religion of Rabelais* (1982, original French edition 1942), called by the author 'an essay on the meaning and spirit of the sixteenth century', Lucien Febvre argued that atheism was not an available option for François Rabelais or for anyone else living in that age. Febvre's concluding chapter was called 'A Century Which Wanted to Believe', and which could not *not* believe. Atheism was indeed much discussed. In England it was said to be the commonest religion of all. He, she or it is an atheist; you are an atheist; but never, 'I am an atheist.'

Whether that was the case or not, and there are those who maintain that Febvre's mind was closed against texts that might have told a different story, there is no doubt that we take a voyage into another country where they do things differently when we try to comprehend the mind-set and worldview of the age of the Reformation. We cannot pick and choose between the beliefs of those early modern Europeans that we find acceptable, and even share, and those that are an embarrassment – even, perhaps especially, for the religious historian, who, if he or she is a believing adherent of one of the mainstream denominations of modern Christianity, is perhaps least qualified to interpret the religious world of the sixteenth century.

It is a matter of warts and all: for example, the Devil, ever present and sometimes materializing as a black dog or some other creature, leaving behind a sulphurous smell. Audiences may have laughed at the character of Dog in a play called *The Witch of Edmonton*, but when an extra devil appeared on the stage in a performance of Christopher Marlowe's *Doctor Faustus* (the 'B' text stage direction reads 'Thunder, and enter the Devils') the actors, let alone the audience, needed counselling. Providence occupied most of the spaces now occupied by 'science' and chance. This was a world that fully expected its end, a world in which the brains of the best mathematicians (including Newton's) were engaged in calculating the most likely date for the Millennium. The most powerful mind of all, that of Joseph Scaliger (1540–1609), was almost unhinged by his efforts to reconcile the discrepant chronologies of the Bible with what other ancient records had to say about the age and history of the earth, a matter of much more than academic embarrassment. Weber asked us to think of the 'disenchantment' of the world. It had not yet happened. We do not belong there. We had better leave.

As everyone knows, the age of the Reformation was also the age of the most extensive prosecution of so-called witchcraft, the 'witch craze'. Conventional chronologies of human progress are disturbed by the fact that it should have been then, and not in 'the Middle Ages', that these atrocities happened. This, too, was part of the Renaissance. It is not true that Protestants specialized in the detection and burning (or, in the case of England and New England, hanging) of witches. Most witches (and most heretics) were killed by catholic governments and it was for the most part in catholic territories that the denunciation of witches spun out of control. In Geneva they were particularly reluctant to jump to conclusions. Medical experts were employed to search the bodies of suspected persons for the Devil's mark, and usually they failed to find it. Other Swiss governments, protestant governments, which favoured zero-tolerance, shook their heads.

Nor did witch beliefs depend much on learned doctrine, whether protestant or catholic. You needed experts to deal with it once it had been turned up out of the local soil, but in the local soil was where it was. Belief in *maleficium* was buried deep in the psyches of individuals and of village communities, which feared and suspected the 'other', who might be and probably was your next-door neighbour. If a hailstorm stripped your vines and not those of your neighbour there had to be a reason. Had not someone seen an old crone down in the stream, passing water through a sieve? The strange sickness that killed your child, or your heifer, was probably connected with the fact that you had turned away from your door a poor old woman looking for relief. This was a world without science, insurance and pharmacology, but which still demanded explanations, and cures. Exploring the anthropology of the subject, Sir Keith Thomas, in the most brilliant of all books on early modern belief, *Religion and the Decline of Magic* (1971), understood it to be part of the process of social modernization. Witchcraft, and popular magic more generally, filled the explanatory and remedial space left vacant by the ecclesiastical magic of the old Catholicism.

Not for long, though. What happened next? Thomas assumed that magic of this kind had a limited shelf-life, withering on the vine by the end of the seventeenth century. Critics advised him to visit Thomas Hardy's Dorset, where it was still alive and well. If the law had allowed it, no doubt Victorian Wessex would have hanged witches as it hanged Tess of the D'Urbevilles. But it did not. Towards the end of the seventeenth century, the clergy were no longer inclined to believe in witchcraft and magistrates were no longer willing to pass down capital sentences. Something had happened, to some mentalities. And that takes us into the age of what one French historian of ideas (Paul Hazard) has called *La crise de la conscience Européene* (translated as *The European Mind, 1680–1715*, 1953). It was a crisis of thinking, and belief, that belongs to another book. Whether the Reformation was simply its cause is a question to hand over to historians of the Enlightenment.

Chronology

1513   Election of Pope Leo X

1514–17   Complutensian Polyglot Bible (only published in 1522)

1515   Luther lectures on St Paul to the Romans

1516   Publication of Erasmus's New Testament in Greek and an original Latin translation, the *Novum Instrumentum*

1517   (31 October) Luther 'posts' the Ninety-Five Theses

1518   (April–May) Disputation at Heidelberg: Luther defends his theology before a chapter meeting of the Augustinian order

(October) Luther meets with Cardinal Cajetan in Augsburg

1519   (June) Election of the emperor Charles V
(July) Leipzig disputation, including the debate between Luther and Johann Eck
(1 January) Huldrych Zwingli begins his ministry at Zürich's Gross Münster

1520   (15 June) Luther threatened with excommunication in the papal bull *Exsurge Domine*
(August/September) Luther publishes the *Address to the Christian Nobility of the German Nation* and *A Prelude on the Babylonian Captivity of the Church*
(November) Luther's treatise *The Freedom of a Christian*
(December) The bull *Exsurge Domine* and the canon law burned in Wittenberg

1521   (January) Luther's excommunication formally pronounced in the bull *Decet Romanum Pontificem*
(April) Diet of Worms
(May) Luther taken to the Wartburg where he remains until March 1522 and where he translates the New Testament
Henry VIII writes *Assertio septem sacramentorum* and is awarded the title of Defender of the Faith by Pope Leo X

1522–3   Religious experiences of Ignatius Loyola at Manresa (near Barcelona) out of which came his *Spiritual Exercises*

1523   Luther writes *Secular Authority: To What Extent It Should Be Obeyed*
Martin Bucer begins his ministry in Strassburg (and with him Wolfgang Capito and Caspar Hedio, joining Matthias Zell)
(January) First public debate about the Reformation in Zürich
(October) Second public debate in Zürich, leading to the removal of images from the churches (June 1524)
Gustavus Vasa begins his reign and a prolonged process of reformation in Sweden

1523–5   Beginnings of the Anabaptist movement in Zürich

1524–5   Peasants' War

1525   (April) End of the Mass in Zürich
(June) Luther marries Katharine von Bora

1526   William Tyndale's English translation of the New Testament printed at Worms
Geneva begins to free itself from Savoyard overlordship, entering into a dependent alliance with Berne

1527   Sack of Rome
The Schleitheim Confession attempts to unite early Anabaptists against 'papists and antipapists'

1528   (January) Public disputation in Berne, leading to the adoption of the Reformation along Zürich lines
Foundation of the Capuchin order (reformed Franciscans)

1529   Iconoclastic riots in Basle
Abolition of the Mass in Strassburg
The so-called Reformation Parliament meets in England (March–April) (second) Diet of Speyer orders the enforcement of the Edict of Worms

(July) The protestation of the Evangelical estates gives us the term 'Protestant'

Colloquy of Marburg; Luther insists on '*hoc est corpus meum*' and refuses to be reconciled to the Zwinglians and Strassburgers

1530 Diet of Augsburg; Confession of Augsburg prepared by Philipp Melanchthon and presented to the diet

1531 Formation of the Schmalkaldic League

Second outbreak of inter-cantonal war in Switzerland: battle of Kapel (11 October) in which Zwingli is killed; Zwingli replaced as *antistes* of Zürich by Heinrich Bullinger

1533 Thomas Cranmer appointed archbishop of Canterbury; Act in Restraint of Appeals, 'this realm of England is an empire'

Cranmer declares the marriage of Henry VIII to Catherine of Aragon to be null and crowns Anne Boleyn queen

1534 Act of Supremacy, acknowledging Henry VIII as supreme head of the English Church

Duke Ulrich restored to the duchy of Württemberg and introduces the Reformation in south Germany

Election of Alessandro Farnese as Pope Paul III, an unlikely reformer

Affair of the 'placards' in Paris leads to religious polarization in France and the emigration of Calvin

1534-5 Anabaptist rule in Münster

1535 Execution of Sir (St) Thomas More

Publication of the first complete English Bible in print

1536 First edition (at Basle) of Calvin's *Institutes*

(May) Geneva undertakes to live 'by the holy law of the gospel'

(July) Calvin arrives in Geneva and is constrained to stay by Guillaume Farel

1536-40 Progressive dissolution of the English monasteries

1537　Calvin presents the Genevan magistrates with the first version of his Ecclesiastical Ordinances
The *Consilium de Emendanda Ecclesia* presented to Paul III
Henrician Reformation introduced into Ireland
Official implementation of the Lutheran Reformation in Denmark under Christian III

1538　Calvin and Farel ordered out of Geneva; Calvin retires to Strassburg

1539　Publication at Strassburg of the second, expanded edition of Calvin's *Institutes*
Publication in England of the officially authorized Great Bible

1539–40　Religious reaction in England: Act of Six Articles and execution of Henry VIII's reforming minister, Thomas Cromwell

1540　Publication in Venice of the *Trattato utilissimo del Beneficio di Jesu Christo crocifisso*
Society of Jesus (the Jesuits) founded by the papal bull *Regimini militantis ecclesiae*

1541　Diet of Regensburg, theological discussions between Lutherans and Cardinal Contarini; near-agreement on doctrine of justification
French edition of Calvin's *Institutes*, the *Institution de la Religion Chrestienne*

1541–2　Calvin returns to Geneva (September 1541) and Calvinist church order established (Ecclesiastical Ordinances, November 1541)

1542　Establishment of the Roman Inquisition by the papal bull *Licet ab initio*

1545　(December) Opening of the Council of Trent

1546–7　Schmalkaldic War

1547　(April) The Council is transferred to Bologna

Accession of Edward VI and the inauguration of a Protestant regime in England

1548 Imperial (or Augsburg) Interim

1549 *Consensus Tigurinus* negotiated between Calvin and Bullinger unites Geneva and Zürich, especially on the doctrine of the Eucharist
First English Prayer Book; Prayer Book Rebellion in the west of England

1551–2 Second session of the Council of Trent

1552 Second (more radically reformed) English Prayer Book

1553 Accession of Mary Tudor in England
Burning of Michael Servetus in Geneva

1555 Religious Peace of Augsburg – *cuius regio, eius religio*
Overthrow of the Perrinist faction and other opponents of Calvin in Geneva
First Geneva-trained pastors dispatched into France
Election of Gian Pietro Carafa as Pope Paul IV
Mary's government begins the burning of heretics in England (Archbishop Cranmer burned at the stake in Oxford, 1556)

1558 (November) Accession of Elizabeth I in England

1559 Foundation of the Geneva Academy
Elizabethan religious settlement in England, also enacted in Ireland
(March) First national synod of the French reformed Churches in Paris
Index of Prohibited Books

1559–60 Definitive editions of Calvin's *Institutes* in Latin and French

1560 Revolution in Scotland; a reformed Church created
Treaty of Edinburgh ends French control of Scotland, preserves the Scottish Reformation and opens the way to a greater 'amity' with England

1562 Outbreak of the first of the Wars of Religion in France

1562–3 Third and final session of the Council of Trent

1563 The Heidelberg Catechism marks the establishment of Calvinism in the Rhenish Palatinate by the Elector Frederick III

1564 Death of Calvin and succession of Theodore Beza as moderator of the Company of Pastors of Geneva

1566–7 'Wonderyear' in the Netherlands; hedge-preaching and iconoclasm

1570 Papal bull *Regnans in excelsis* excommunicates Elizabeth I

1572 Election of Pope Gregory XIII
Massacre of St Bartholomew

1575 Formalization of St Philip Neri's Congregation of the Oratory

1577 Formula of Concord unites German Lutherans

1580 Book of Concord

1581 Penal laws passed against Roman Catholics in England

1585 Election of Pope Sixtus V

1587 (February) Execution of Mary, Queen of Scots

1589 Assassination of French King Henry III; accession of Henry of Navarre as Henry IV contested by Catholic League

1593 Henry IV converts to Catholicism – 'Paris is worth a Mass'

1598 Pacification of Nantes ends the French Wars of Religion

1603 Death of Elizabeth I and accession of James VI of Scotland as James I of England

1605 Gunpowder Plot in England

1618–19 Synod of Dort (Dordrecht) deals with divisions in the
         Reformed Churches in the Netherlands and elsewhere
         on the doctrine of grace

1618 Outbreak of the Thirty Years' War

1642 Outbreak of the English Civil War

1649 Execution of Charles I

1648 Peace of Westphalia

1688–9 'Glorious Revolution' in England; deposition of the
        Catholic James II and subsequent legislation secures the
        Protestant settlement in the British Isles

Suggestions for further reading

FOR REFERENCE AND DOCUMENTATION

F. L. Cross and E. A. Livingstone, eds, *The Oxford Dictionary of the Christian Church*, 3rd edn (Oxford, 1997); A. G. Dickens and J. M. Tonkin, *The Reformation in Historical Thought* (Oxford, 1985); M. Greengrass, *The European Reformation c.1500–1618* (London and New York, 1998) (an indispensable mine of chronology and other factual information); A. Hastings et al., eds, *The Oxford Companion to Christian Thought* (Oxford, 2000); H. J. Hillerbrand, ed., *The Oxford Encyclopedia of the Reformation*, 4 vols (New York and Oxford, 1996); G. Muller, ed., *Theologische Realenzyklopedie* (Berlin, 1976–); D. J. Ziegler, ed., *Great Debates of the Reformation* (New York, 1969).

General and Chapter One: Reformation, what Reformation?

J. Bossy, *Christianity in the West 1400–1700* (Oxford, 1985); E. Cameron, *The European Reformation* (Oxford, 1991); O. Chadwick, *The Early Reformation on the Continent*, Oxford History of the Christian Church (Oxford, 2001); A. Cunningham and O. P. Grell, *The Four Horsemen of the Apocalpyse* (Cambridge, 2001); J. Delumeau, *Le Catholicisme entre Luther et Voltaire* (Paris, 1971), English translation, *Catholicism Between Luther and Voltaire*, without the bibliography (London, 1978); G. R. Elton, *Reformation Europe 1517–1559*, 2nd edn, Blackwell Classic Histories of Europe (Oxford, 1985); F. Fernández-Armesto and Derek Wilson, *Reformation: Christianity and the World 1500–2000* (London, 1996); E. G. Léonard, *Histoire générale du Protestantisme*, 2 vols (Paris, 1951). English translation, J. M. H. Reid and E. R. M. Bethell, *A History of Protestantism*, 2 vols (London, 1967); Diarmaid MacCulloch, *Reformation: Europe's House Divided 1490–1700* (London 2003); A. Pettegree, ed., *The Early Reformation in*

Europe (Cambridge, 1992); A. Pettegree, ed., *The Reformation World* (London and New York, 2000); R. W. Scribner et al., eds, *The Reformation in National Context* (Cambridge, 1994); R. W. Scribner, *The German Reformation* (Basingstoke, 1986); J. D. Tracy, *Europe's Reformations 1450–1650* (Lanham, Md, and Oxford, 1999).

Chapter Two: The late medieval Church and its Reformation

E. Cameron, *The Reformation of the Heretics: The Waldenses of the Alps 1480–1580* (Oxford, 1984); E. Delaruelle, E. R. Labande and P. Ourliac, *L'Église au temps du Grande Scisme et la crise conciliaire*, Fliche et Martin, *Histoire de l'église*, vol. 15 (Paris, 1952–5); E. Duffy, *Saints and Sinners: A History of the Popes* (New Haven and London, 1997); A. Hudson, *The Premature Reformation: Wycliffite Texts and Lollard History* (Oxford, 1988); A. E. McGrath, *The Intellectual Origins of the European Reformation* (Oxford, 1987); H. A. Oberman, *The Harvest of Late Medieval Theology: Gabriel Biel and Late Medieval Nominalism* (Cambridge, Mass., 1963); H. A. Oberman, *The Dawn of the Reformation* (Edinburgh, 1986); L. Pastor, *History of the Popes from the Close of the Middle Ages*, 40 vols (London, 1912–52); R. R. Post, *The Modern Devotion*, Studies in Medieval and Reformation Thought, 3 (Leiden, 1968); R. W. Southern, *The Western Church in the Later Middle Ages* (Ithaca, NY, and London, 1970); G. Strauss, *Pre-Reformation Germany* (London, 1972); G. Strauss, ed., *Manifestations of Discontent in Germany on the Eve of the Reformation* (Bloomington, Ind., 1972); T. N. Tentler, *Sin and Confession on the Eve of the Reformation* (Princeton, NJ, 1977); J. Toussaert, *Le sentiment religieux en Flandre à la fin du moyen-age* (Paris, 1963); C. Trinkhaus and H. A. Oberman, eds, *The Pursuit of Holiness in Late Medieval and Renaissance Religion* (Leiden, 1974); J. A. F. Thompson, *Popes and Princes 1417–1517: Politics and Polity in the Late Medieval Church* (London, 1980); W. Ullmann, *The Origins of the Great Schism* (London, 1948).

Chapter Three: Words, language and books

D. Daniell, *William Tyndale: A Biography* (New Haven and London, 1994); E. Eisenstein, *The Printing Press as an Agent of Change*, 2 vols

(Cambridge, 1979); A. Fox, *Oral and Literate Culture in England 1500–1700* (Oxford, 2000); L. Febvre et H. J. Martin, *L'apparition du livre* (Paris, 1958), English translation, D. Gerard, *The Coming of the Book: The Impact of Printing, 1450–1800* (London, 1976); J.-F. Gilmont, ed., *La Réforme et le livre: l'Europe de l'imprimé (1517–v.1570)* (Paris, 1990), English translation, K. Maag, *The Reformation and the Book* (Aldershot and Brookfield, Vt, 1998); A. Hastings, *The Construction of Nationhood: Ethnicity, Religion and Nationalism* (Cambridge, 1997); J. Mueller, *The Native Tongue and the Word: Developments in English Prose Style 1380–1580* (Chicago and London, 1984); L. W. Spitz, *The Religious Renaissance of the German Humanists* (Cambridge, Mass., 1963); G. Strauss, *Luther's House of Learning: Indoctrination of the Young in the German Reformation* (Baltimore and London, 1978); B. Vickers, ed., *English Renaissance Literary Criticism* (Oxford, 1999).

ERASMUS:

TEXTS: P. H. Allen, ed., *Opus Epistolarum Desiderii Erasmi Roterodami*, 12 vols (Oxford, 1906–47) (Erasmus's collected correspondence, an indispensable source); *Collected Works of Erasmus*, in English translation (Toronto, 1974–); *Colloquies*, translated C. R. Thompson (Chicago, 1965); *Adages*, translated M. M. Phillips and R. A. B. Mynors (Toronto, 1982–).

BIOGRAPHIES AND STUDIES: R. Bainton, *Erasmus of Christendom* (New York, 1969; Tring, 1988); P. G. Bietenholz and T. B. Deutscher, *Contemporaries of Erasmus: A Biographical Register of Renaissance and Reformation*, 3 vols (Toronto, 1985); J. K. McConica, *Erasmus* (Oxford, 1991).

Chapter Four: Luther discovers the gospel and challenges the Church

LUTHER:

WRITINGS: *Werke: Kritische Gesamtausgabe*, c.100 vols (Weimar, 1883–1997) (always referred to as the 'Weimarer Ausgabe', or simply 'WA'); *Luther's Works: American Edition*, ed. J. Pelikan and H. T. Lehmann, 55 vols (St Louis, Mo., and Philadelphia, 1955–) (not exhaustive); E. G. Rupp and B. J. Drewery, *Martin Luther* (London,

1970); I. D. K. Siggins, *Luther* (Edinburgh, 1972); H. Wace and C. Buchheim, *Luther's Primary Works* (London, 1896).

BIOGRAPHIES AND STUDIES: R. H. Bainton, *Here I Stand: A Life of Martin Luther* (New York, 1950); E. Bizer, *Fides ex auditu: Eine Untersuchungen über die Entdeckung der Gerechtigkeit Gottes durch Martin Luther* (Neukirchen, 1958); H. Bornhamm, *Martin Luther in der Mittes seines Leben* (Göttingen, 1979), English translation, E. T. Bachmann, *Luther in Mid-Career* (London, 1983); A. G. Dickens, *The German Nation and Martin Luther* (London, 1974); G. Ebeling, *Luther: Einführung in sein Denken* (Tubingen, 1964), English translation, R. A. Wilson, *Luther: An Introduction to His Thought* (London, 1970); E. H. Erikson, *Young Man Luther: A Study in Psychoanalysis and History* (New York, 1993); E. Iserloh, *The Theses Were Not Posted* (London, 1968); R. Marius, *Martin Luther: The Christian Between God and Death* (Cambridge, Mass., 1999); H. A. Oberman, *Luther: Mensch zwischen Gott und Teufel* (Berlin, 1982), English translation, E. Walliser-Schwarzbart, *Luther: Man between God and the Devil* (New Haven and London, 1989); E. G. Rupp, *The Righteousness of God: Luther Studies* (London, 1953) E. G. Rupp, *Luther's Progress to the Diet of Worms* (London, 1951); I. D. K. Siggins, *Luther and His Mother* (Philadelphia, 1981); U. Saarnivaara, *Luther Discovers the Gospel* (St Louis, Mo., 1951); D. E. Steinmetz, *Luther and Staupitz: An Essay in the Intellectual Origins of the Protestant Reformation* (Durham, N.C., 1980). Many hundreds of further titles will be found in the annually published *Luther-Jahrbuch* (1919–).

Chapter Five: Alternative patterns of reformation

GENERAL:
E. G. Rupp, *Patterns of Reformation* (London, 1969); B. Gordon, *The Swiss Reformation* (Manchester, 2002).

KARLSTADT AND MÜNTZER:
R. J. Sider, *Andreas Bodenstein von Karlstadt: The Development of His Thought* (Leiden, 1974); Müntzer's *Works*, English translation, P. E. Matheson (Edinburgh, 1988); E. Gritsch, *Reformer without a Church: The Life and Thought of Thomas Müntzer* (Philadelphia, 1967);

T. Scott, *Thomas Müntzer: Theology and Revolution in the German Reformation* (Basingstoke, 1989).

ZWINGLI AND ZÜRICH:
C. W. Bromiley, ed., *Zwingli and Bullinger: Selected Writings*, Library of Christian Classics (Philadelphia, 1953); G. R. Potter *Zwingli* (Cambridge, 1976).

BUCER AND STRASSBURG:
M. U. Chrisman, *Strasbourg and the Reform* (New Haven, 1967); H. Eells, *Martin Bucer* (New Haven, 1931).

ANABAPTISTS:
Mennonite Quarterly Review and *Mennonite Enclyclopedia* are essential works of reference; C. P. Clasen, *Anabaptism: A Social History 1525–1618* (Ithaca and London, 1972); H.-J. Goertz, *Die Taufer: Geschichte und Deutung* (Munich, 1988); J. M. Stayer, *Anabaptists and the Sword* (Lawrence, 1976); G. H. Williams, ed., *Spiritual and Anabaptist Writers*, Library of Christian Classics (London, 1957); G. H. Williams, *The Radical Reformation* (London, 1962; 2nd revised edn, Kirksville, Mo., 1992).

Chapter Six: Calvin and Calvinism

TEXTS:
Calvin's *Opera*, in *Corpus Reformatorum*, 59 vols, ed. G. Baum, E. Cunitz and E. Reuss (Braunschweig and Berlin, 1853–1900); Calvin's *Institutes*, English translation, F. L. Battles, ed. J. T. McNeill, Library of Christian Classics (London, 1960); *Theological Treatises*, ed. J. K. S. Reid, Library of Christian Classics (London, 1954); *Correspondance de Théodore de Bèze*, ed. A. Dufour et al. (Geneva, 1960–); *Registres de la compagnie des pasteurs de Genève* (Geneva, 1962–); documents in A. Duke, G. Lewis and A. Pettegree, *Calvinism in Europe 1540–1610* (Manchester and New York, 1992), and G. R. Potter and M. Greengrass, eds, *John Calvin* (London, 1983).

BIOGRAPHIES AND STUDIES: P. Benedict, *Christ's Churches Purely Reformed: A Social History of Calvinism* (New Haven and London, 2002); William J. Bouwsma, *John Calvin: A Sixteenth-Century Portrait*

(Oxford, 1988); F. Higman, *The Style of John Calvin in His French Polemical Treatises* (Oxford, 1957); H. Hopfl, *The Christian Polity of John Calvin* (Cambridge, 1982); R. Kingdon, *Geneva and the Coming of the Wars of Religion in France, 1555–1563* (Geneva, 1956); W. Monter, *Calvin's Geneva* (New York, 1967); T. H. L. Parker, *John Calvin* (London, 1975); W. G. Naphy, *Calvin and the Consolidation of the Genevan Reformation* (Manchester, 1994); A. Pettegree, A. Duke and G. Lewis, eds, *Calvinism in Europe 1540–1620* (Cambridge, 1994); M. Prestwich, ed., *International Calvinism 1541–1715* (Oxford, 1985).

Chapter Seven: Counter-Reformation

J. Bossy, 'The Counter-Reformation and the People of Catholic Europe', *Past & Present*, no. 47 (1970); A. G. Dickens, *The Counter Reformation* (London, 1968); H. O. Evennett, ed. J. Bossy, *The Spirit of the Counter-Reformation* (Cambridge, 1968); D. Fenlon, *Heresy and Obedience in Tridentine Italy: Cardinal Pole and the Counter Reformation* (Cambridge, 1972); R. Po-Chia Hsia, *The World of Catholic Renewal, 1540–1770* (Cambridge, 1998); J. Hook, *The Sack of Rome* (London, 1972); H. Jedin, *Geschichte des Konzils von Trient*, 4 vols (Freiburg im Breisgau, 1949–75), English translation, E. Graf, *A History of the Council of Trent*, 2 vols (London, 1957, 1961); H. Jedin, *Krisis und Abschluss des Trienter Konzils 1562/3* (Freiburg, 1964), English translation, *Crisis and Closure of the Council of Trent* (London, 1967); H. Jedin, *Katholische Reformation oder Gegenreformation?* (Lucerne, 1946); P. McNair, *Peter Martyr in Italy: An Anatomy of Apostacy* (Oxford, 1967); J. W. O'Malley, *The First Jesuits* (Cambridge, Mass., 1993); P. Matheson, *Cardinal Contarini at Regensburg* (Oxford, 1972); H. J. Schroeder, ed., *The Canons and Decrees of the Council of Trent* (Rockford, Ill., 1978).

Chapter Eight: Exceptional cases: the Reformation in the British Isles

P. Collinson, *The Religion of Protestants: The Church in English Society, 1559–1625* (Oxford, 1983); I. B. Cowan, *The Scottish Reformation: Church and Society in Sixteenth-Century Scotland* (London,

1982); A. G. Dickens, *The English Reformation*, 2nd edn (London, 1989); G. Donaldson, *The Scottish Reformation* (Cambridge, 1960); E. Duffy, *The Stripping of the Altars: Traditional Religion in England c.1400–c.1580* (New Haven and London, 1992); C. Haigh, *English Reformations: Religion, Politics and Society under the Tudors* (Oxford, 1993); D. MacCulloch, *Thomas Cranmer: A Life* (New Haven and London, 1996); D. MacCulloch, *Tudor Church Militant: Edward VI and the Protestant Reformation* (London, 1999); D. MacCulloch, *The Later Reformation in England, 1547–1603*, 2nd edn (Basingstoke, 2001); T. W. Moody, F. X. Martin and F. J. Byrne, eds, *A New History of Ireland*, vol. III, *Early Modern Ireland*, 2nd edn (Oxford, 1991); M. Todd, *The Culture of Protestantism in Early Modern Scotland* (New Haven and London, 2002); G. Williams, *Wales and the Reformation* (Cardiff, 1997).

Chapter Nine: Politics

T. A. Brady, *The Politics of the Reformation in Germany: Jacob Sturm (1489–1553) of Strasbourg* (Atlantic Highlands, N.J., 1997); J. H. Burns, ed., *The Cambridge History of Political Thought 1450–1700* (Cambridge, 1991); W. D. J. Cargill Thompson, *The Political Thought of Martin Luther* (Brighton, 1984); F. L. Carsten, *Princes and Parliaments in Germany from the Fifteenth to the Eighteenth Century* (Oxford 1959); H. J. Cohn, *Government in Reformation Europe 1520–1560* (London, 1971); C. Scott Dixon, *The Reformation in Germany* (Oxford, 2002); A. Duke, *Reformation and Revolt in the Low Countries* (London and Ronceverte, W. Va., 1990); R. Evans, *The Making of the Habsburg Monarchy 1550–1700* (Oxford, 1979); M. Greengrass, *The French Reformation* (Oxford, 1987); O. P. Grell, ed., *The Scandinavian Reformation* (Cambridge, 1995); J. Guy, *Tudor England* (Oxford, 1988); D. R. Kelley, *The Beginning of Ideology: Consciousness and Society in the French Reformation* (Cambridge, 1981); H. G. Koenigsberger, *Estates and Revolutions: Essays in Early Modern European History* (Ithaca and London, 1971); K. Maag, ed., *The Reformation in Eastern and Central Europe* (Aldershot, 1997); R. Mason, ed., *John Knox and the British Reformations* (Aldershot and Brookfield, Vt, 1998); B. Moeller, *Reichstadt und Reformation*, updated edn (Berlin, 1987),

English translation, H. C. Erik Midelfort and M. U. Edwards, *Imperial Cities and the Reformation* (Philadelphia, 1972); S. Ozment, *The Reformation in the Cities* (New Haven, 1975); J. J. Scarisbrick, *Henry VIII* (London, 1968); R. W. Scribner, 'Paradigms of Urban Reformation: Gemeindereformation or Erastian Reformation', *in* Leif Grane and Kai Horby, eds, *The Danish Reformation Against Its International Background* (Göttingen, 1990); Q. R. D. Skinner, *The Foundations of Modern Political Thought*, vol. II, *The Age of the Reformation* (Cambridge, 1978); G. Strauss, *Nuremberg in the Sixteenth Century* (New York, 1966).

Chapter Ten: People

L. J. Abray, *The People's Reformation: Magistrates, Clergy and Commons in Strasbourg 1500–1598* (Oxford, 1985); P. Bickle, *Die revolution von 1525*, revised edn (Munich, 1981), English translation, T. A. Brady Jr, and H. C. Erik Midelfort, *The Revolution of 1525* (Baltimore, 1981); G. Franz, *Der deutsch Bauernkrieg*, 11th edn (Darmstadt, 1977); R. Houlbrooke, *Death, Religion and the Family in England 1480–1750* (Oxford, 1998); *Luther's Works*, American edn, Vols 44–7, *The Christian in Society* (Philadelphia, 1962–71); S. Ozment, *When Fathers Ruled: Family Life in Reformation Europe* (Cambridge, Mass., 1983); L. Roper, *The Holy Household: Women and Morals in Reformation Augsburg* (Oxford, 1989); T. Scott and B. Scribner, eds, *The German Peasants' War: A History in Documents* (Atlantic Highlands, N.J., 1991); R. W. Scribner, *For the Sake of Simple Folk: Popular Propaganda for the German Reformation* (Cambridge, 1981); R. W. Scribner, *Popular Culture and Popular Movements in Reformation Germany* (London and Ronceverte, Vt, 1987); J. M. Stayer, *The German Peasants' War and Anabaptist Community of Goods* (Montreal, 1991).

Chapter Eleven: Art

M. Aston, *England's Iconoclasts: Laws Against Images* (Oxford, 1988); C. C. Christensen, *Art and the Reformation in Germany* (Athens, Oh.,

1979); P. Collinson, *The Birthpangs of Protestant England: Religious and Cultural Change in the Sixteenth and Seventeenth Centuries* (Basingstoke, 1988); T. Cooper, ed., *The Journal of William Dowsing: Iconoclasm in East Anglia During the English Civil War* (Woodbridge, 2001); P. M. Crew, *Calvinist Preaching and Iconoclasm in the Netherlands 1544–1569* (Cambridge, 1978); C. M. N. Eire, *War Against the Idols: The Reformation of Worship from Erasmus to Calvin* (Cambridge, 1986); Charles Garside Jr., *Zwingli and the Arts* (New Haven and London, 1966); P. Le Huray, *Music and the Reformation in England, 1549–1660*, 2nd edn (London, 1978); D. Loades, ed., *John Foxe and the English Reformation* (Aldershot and Brookfield, Vt, 1997); J. North, *The Ambassadors' Secret: Holbein and the World of the Renaissance* (London and New York, 2002); E. Panofsky, *The Life and Art of Albrecht Dürer*, 4th edn (Princeton, 1971); A. Saunders, *The Sixteenth-Century French Emblem Book* (Geneva, 1988); T. Watt, *Cheap Print and Popular Piety, 1550–1640* (Cambridge, 1991); D. Wilson, *Hans Holbein: Portrait of an Unknown Man* (London, 1997).

Chapter Twelve: A Reformation watershed? (highly selective)

THE WEBER THESIS:

Max Weber, *Die protestantische Ethik und der Geist des Kapitalismus*, first published in volumes 20 and 21 of *Archiv fur Sozialwissenschaft und Sozialpolitik* (1904–5), reprinted in 1920 in Gesämmelte Aufsätze zur Religionsoziologie, English translation, Talcott Parsons, *The Protestant Ethic and the Spirit of Capitalism* (London, 1930); S. N. Eisenstadt, ed., *The Protestant Ethic and Modernization* (New York and London, 1968); H. Lehmann and G. Roth, eds, *Weber's Protestant Ethic: Origins, Evidence, Contexts* (New York, 1993).

CONFESSIONALIZATION, THE SECOND REFORMATION AND EVANGELICALISM:

B. Nischan, *Lutherans and Calvinists in the Age of Confessionalism* (Aldershot, 1999); W. Reinhard and H. Schilling, eds, *Die Katholische Konfessionalisierung* (Münster, 1995); H. Schilling, ed., *Die reformierte Konfessionalisierung in Deutschland: Das Problem der 'zweiten Reformation'* (Gutersloh, 1987); H. Schilling, *Religion, Political Culture and* the *Emergence of Early Modern Society* (Leiden, 1992); J. Scott, *England's Troubles: Seventeenth-Century English Political Instability in European Context* (Cambridge, 2000); F. E. Stoeffler, *The Rise of Evangelical Pietism* (Leiden, 1965); N. Tyacke, *Anti-Calvinists: The Rise of English Arminianism c.1590–1640*, 2nd edn (Oxford, 1990); W. R. Ward, *The Protestant Evangelical Awakening* (Cambridge, 1992).

CONTINUITIES, DISCONTINUITIES AND THE DISENCHANTMENT OF THE WORLD:

J. Bossy, *Peace in the Post-Reformation* (Cambridge, 1998); K. Thomas, *Religion and the Decline of Magic* (London, 1973); A. Walsham, *Providence in Early Modern England* (Oxford, 1999).

WITCHCRAFT:

R. Briggs, *Witches and Neighbours: The Social and Cultural Context of European Witchcraft* (London, 1996); S. Clark, *Thinking with Demons: The Idea of Witchcraft in Early Modern Europe* (Oxford, 1997); H. C. Erik Midelfort, *Witch-Hunting in Southwestern Germany, 1562–1684* (Stanford, 1972); E. W. Monter, *Witchcraft in France and Switzerland* (London, 1976).

UNBELIEF, SCEPTICISM, TOLERANCE AND INTOLERANCE AND THE BIRTH OF THE ENLIGHTENMENT:

L. Febvre, *Le problème de l'incroyance au XVIᵉ siècle*, 2nd edn (Paris, 1988), English translation, B. Gottlieb, *The Problem of Unbelief in the Sixteenth Century: The Religion of Rabelais* (Cambridge, Mass., 1982); O. P. Grell and R. W. Scribner, eds, *Tolerance and Intolerance in the European Reformation* (Cambridge, 1996); P. Hazard, *La crise de la conscience européene, 1680–1715*, 3 vols (Paris, 1935), English translation, J. L. May (London, 1954); H. T. Mason, *Pierre Bayle and Voltaire* (Oxford, 1963); R. H. Popkin, *The History of Scepticism from Erasmus to Spinoza* (Berkeley, 1979).

Index